MARY

and the Christian Life

SCRIPTURAL REFLECTIONS
ON THE FIRST DISCIPLE

MARY

and the Christian Life

SCRIPTURAL REFLECTIONS
ON THE FIRST DISCIPLE

Amy Welborn

theWORD
among us®
press

Also by Amy Welborn

The Loyola Kids Book of Saints
The Loyola Kids Book of Heroes
The Words We Pray: Discovering the Richness of Traditional
   Catholic Prayer
A Catholic Woman's Book of Days
The *Prove It!* series of apologetics for youth
Here. Now. A Catholic Guide to the Good Life
De-coding Da Vinci: The Facts Behind the Fiction of the
   Da Vinci Code
De-coding Mary Magdalene: Truth, Legend, and Lies

Published by The Word Among Us Press
9639 Doctor Perry Road
Ijamsville, Maryland 21754
www.wordamongus.org
ISBN: 978-1-59325-113-0
12 11 10 09 08 1 2 3 4 5

Cover design by John Hamilton Design
Raphael (Raffaello Sanzio) (1483–1520)
Madonna del Granduca (Madonna of the Grandduke). 1506. Oil on wood
Location: Galleria Palatina, Palazzo Pitti, Florence, Italy
Photo Credit: Scala/Art Resource, NY
Text design by David Crosson

Unless otherwise noted Scripture citations are from the New Revised Standard
Version Bible: Catholic Edition, copyright ©1989 by the Division of Christian
Education of the National Council of the Churches of Christ in the United
States of America. All rights reserved. Used with permission.
Additional acknowledgments on page 151.

Library of Congress Cataloging-in-Publication Data
Welborn, Amy.
  Mary and the Christian life : scriptural reflections on the first disciple / Amy
Welborn.
      p. cm.
  Includes bibliographical references (p.   ).
  ISBN 978-1-59325-113-0
  1. Mary, Blessed Virgin, Saint--Devotion to. 2. Christian life--Catholic authors.
I. Title.
  BT645.W45 2008
  232.91--dc22
                              2008001341

Contents

We fly to your patronage,
O holy Mother of God;
despise not our petitions
in our necessities,
but from all dangers
deliver us always,
O glorious and blessed Virgin.

—*Sub Tuum Praesidium* (third-century Egyptian papyrus)

Introduction

Imagine Christianity without Mary.

Just try.

Of course, in one sense it's quite impossible, since Christianity is about Jesus, word-made-flesh, born of a virgin. You can't have the Christian story without that.

For a moment, though, move beyond the simple facts of history. Consider your understanding of what it means to be a disciple of Jesus, living, worshipping, and serving him in this world and hoping for eternal life in the next.

Imagine trying to do that without Mary in the room.

Even if Mary doesn't play a huge role in your devotional or spiritual life, the results of that mental exercise might surprise you.

Why is that? What is missing when we take Mary out of the picture?

Simple. We are. Without Mary, we risk Christianity becoming nothing more than an idea.

The devotion to Mary that is so important to Catholicism and Orthodoxy is rich and complex. It can be—and has been—explored in theological, spiritual, psychological, cultural, mythological, and literary terms. No woman has been written about more; no woman has been imagined or invoked more.

That's astonishing when you remember who we are talking about: a Jewish woman who lived in the backwaters of the Roman Empire two thousand years ago. A nobody, it would seem, logically speaking. Humanly speaking.

How many women lived two thousand years ago? Plenty.

How many Jewish women lived in Galilee? Several. But we remember *her*. We venerate and honor her. We name our children and churches after her. We hang her image around our necks and in our homes. We call her Our Lady, Our Mother.

But why is that? What do we see in her? What hopes are met in her story? What truths does she embody for us? What has she done for us?

Is she a mirror?

A window?

A door?

This book explores that question, but not in an abstract way. Although it touches on historical questions, it's not a history or apologetics book. Nor is it a work of theology or an expert examination of spiritual, typological, or mythological themes.

Mary and the Christian Life is simply an exploration of what the title implies. As disciples of Jesus, we all are committed to deepening that relationship every day we're on earth. We seek to open ourselves more completely to whatever it is Jesus would have us do here, to live so that it is no longer myself but Christ who lives in me for the sake of the world—the whole world. That's the Christian life (Galatians 2:19-20).

Mary can help us on that journey. Like all the saints, she can help us through her example and through her prayers. But of course she is not like any other saint in one important way: the way she is related to Jesus. She is his mother. She carried him in her womb, cared for him as her baby, child, and adult son, and as his mother, watched him die and cared for his dead body—the same body she had borne within her.

So there is something more about Mary, something vital in her that is accessible to us whether we are a man or a woman, whether or not we have ever been married or had children.

Mary Brings Us Christ's Nearness

Without Mary we are doomed to live according to our own ideas, our own inadequate understanding, our own reductive way of looking at things. And when this happens, Jesus himself becomes an abstraction. The only thing that saves us from the temptation of making him who was "begotten, not made" according to our own image is the presence of his Mother. Mary visits us to bring us Christ's nearness.

—Peter John Cameron, OP, *Magnificat,* May 2007

The Church Journeys on the Path of Mary

Strengthened by the presence of Christ (see Matthew 28:20), the Church journeys through time towards the consummation of the ages and goes to meet the Lord who comes. But on this journey—and I wish to make this point straightaway—she proceeds along the path already trodden by the Virgin Mary, who "advanced in her pilgrimage of faith, and loyally persevered in her union with her Son unto the cross."

—Pope John Paul II, *Redemptoris Mater,* 2

We have few moments of Mary's life recorded in Scripture, but each one of them seems to have the power to speak to us, because each of them mirrors moments in the life of every disciple of Jesus: moments in which we hear good news, respond, praise, ponder, suffer, and rejoice.

These moments, these sketches of Mary, scattered through the gospels, are not simply glimpses of how to meet a challenge, be faithful, or maintain hope in adversity in general terms. They're not scenes from a greeting card or a motivational poster. They are about Mary's very specific relationship to Jesus.

Mary's relationship to Jesus is anything but abstract. It is the most concrete relationship between two people we can imagine—a mother and her child. As we consider Mary, as we get to know her better, as we immerse ourselves in her story and the story of God's presence among her people, the people of Israel, the story of our own faith grows deeper roots, opens up, and at the same time startles us with its intimacy.

The reason, then, why it is so strange to us to even imagine a Christianity without Mary is because our faith in Jesus isn't abstract, either. Jesus isn't God become an idea, a concept, a picture, a myth, or an ideal. Jesus is God become human, in this world, for this world. For us. God Made Man in the midst of our human existence.

How can that be? What does it mean? When God dwells among us, what next? Mary's very concrete, very real relationship with Jesus points us to the answers—answers that allow us to open our own lives in our own version of Mary's *fiat*.

Too often, when we are presented with the whole concept of religion, we experience an almost reflexive word association. They say "religion;" we think "have to." Even the best-intentioned of us can be tempted to associate elements of obligation with our religious commitment. What do we *have to* believe about Mary, we wonder? Why *must* we hassle with these teachings, this presence of Mary?

It might be more helpful and more true to the reality of how the Christian faith came to us and developed over the millennia if we tried to shift our paradigms. Devotion to Mary in Christianity was not imposed from above by religious authorities. There were no commissions that planned out the structure of the rosary and then forced the unwilling to recite it. (Devotions to Mary that developed over the centuries are described at the end of each chapter.) This woman's presence as such a favorite companion on the Christian journey wasn't mandated or legislated.

No. What happened is that Mary's story and identity had its own power that moved Christians from very early on. They found that their faith in Jesus was deepened and strengthened when they consciously invoked Mary as their companion, for in Mary they discovered that the human being who knew Jesus most intimately was one of them.

It is hard enough to understand the mystery of God. God, all-powerful, eternal, all-knowing Truth and Love (and sometimes it is that last aspect that is most mysterious of all to us), so far above us, yet knowing our hearts better than we ever could. How can we know him?

God knows this, and because he does, and because he loves, he comes among us as one of us, speaking our language, touching us, feeding us, laughing and weeping with us, suffering alongside us, dying.

Another mystery all its own. We see God among us, our creator come to redeem us from our sin and give us life. But how are we to respond? What do we say? What do we do?

Enter the girl from Nazareth.

"Rejoice!"

Instead of seeing Mary, on the one hand, as a set of doctrines and on the other, as a set of interesting devotional practices, perhaps we could see her as she is: a gift from the God who knows our limitations, our dilemmas, and our fears. A God who chooses to be conceived within the womb of a woman whose presence, response, words, and actions can help us live out the concrete reality of faith in the One she so concretely bore within her womb, and followed with her eyes and heart the rest of his earthly life.

So what does Mary have to do with the Christian life? Quite a bit. As a disciple, as a pilgrim, she shows us how to respond to God's surprising grace and faithful promise. But she is more than an example. As millions of Christians throughout history have found, Mary doesn't only walk ahead of us. She walks *with* us as well.

CHAPTER I

Who Is Mary?

*God puts the destiny of all mankind in a young
woman's hands.*
—Pope John Paul II, General Audience, September 18, 1996

First things first: what do we know about Mary?

Historically, not as much as we might like. That can be frustrating for us, accustomed as we are to modern biographies that tell us everything we want to know—and sometimes what we don't—about historical figures.

So it's important to remember that our sources for information about Mary, the gospels, are not biographies. Biographies certainly were written during the first century—Plutarch was a first-century Greek who wrote the very famous *Lives*—so if biography had been the plain and simple purpose of these documents, that's what they would have been called. But they weren't. From the beginning, as far as we know, they were thought of as "gospels."

The word "gospel" is a derivation of an old English phrase "godspell," which means "good news." It was *evangelium* in Latin, and the authors of these works that told of good news are called the evangelists: Matthew, Mark, Luke, and John.

When we are searching through these documents for historical information, we can't forget that their purpose isn't to satisfy our twenty-first-century curiosity about facts and figures. Their purpose is to show us why we should believe the good news that Jesus of Nazareth, son of Mary, is the Messiah and Lord, the Son of God.

To the extent that Mary plays a role in bringing that good news into the world and illuminates its meaning, she's there.

Miriam of Nazareth

We call her "Mary," but she was probably called either "Maryam" or "Miriam" by those who knew her. We can't commit to one or the other because we don't know what language the Jewish residents of Galilee would have spoken. It might have been a form of Aramaic, or it might have been Hebrew. We're really not sure.

Jesus was born about 6–7 B.C. Yes, you read that right. It's complicated, but because of adjustments to the calendar in the Middle Ages, we now know that what was traditionally noted as "0"—the year Jesus was born—was actually a few years earlier.

So, if we accept that date of Jesus' birth and work from the traditional assumption that Mary was in her early teens at the time of Jesus' birth, we can settle her own birth year as somewhere between 20 and perhaps 23 B.C.

Mary's birth is celebrated on September 8, which is interesting because, if you think about it, it's unusual to celebrate the birthdays of saints. We usually celebrate their birth into eternal life—their deaths. But with Mary and John the Baptist (June 24), we also remember their births, because these two figures played a direct role in the coming of the Savior.

The Bible tells us nothing about Mary's family of origin, except to say that Elizabeth, the mother of John the Baptist, was a relation of hers. While Matthew and Luke both include genealogies in their gospels, the family line is Joseph's, affirming Jesus' association through his foster father with the house of David.

Stepping outside of Scripture, we find a bit more, some parts of which might be familiar to you.

Early Christians produced more texts than those we find in the New Testament. Those that were selected for inclusion in the canon of Scripture met certain criteria: 1. They had apostolic origins. That is, they could be traced back to the earliest era of Christianity; 2. What they expressed was consistent with the "rule of faith" taught by Jesus to the apostles and then handed down; and 3. They were suitable for proclaiming anywhere in worship. In other words, they didn't have any particular local angle that would make them uninteresting or unhelpful to Christians in various parts of the world.

We actually have quite a few non-canonical Christian texts from the late first and second centuries that reveal the beliefs and practices of the early disciples of Jesus. Some of them are clearly reflective of the life of early Christians. *The Didache* is a good example and well worth reading today. Others are more puzzling to the modern reader and seem to contain not only some snippets of history but legends as well.

One of these is the *Proto-Evangelium of James*, also known as the *Infancy Narrative of James*. Most scholars believe that it dates from the mid-second century, with the earliest manuscript we have being from the third century. It quotes big chunks of both Matthew and Luke but also has quite a few chapters that you're not going to find anywhere else. Most of that material is about Mary.

This book identifies Mary's parents as Joachim and Anne, or Anna. It's also in this book that we read stories of Mary's early life—that she was born in Jerusalem in answer to her aged mother's prayer. In thanksgiving for Mary's conception, Anne dedicated her to the Temple in Jerusalem; and it was there, from

MARY'S FOREMOTHERS

Today a list of women is admired: Sarah is acclaimed as the fertile field of peoples; Rebekah is honored as the able conciliator of blessings; Leah, too, is admired as mother of the ancestor [Judah] according to the flesh; Deborah is praised for having struggled beyond the powers of her womanly nature; Elizabeth is called blessed for having carried the Forerunner, who leapt for joy in her womb, and for having given witness to grace; Mary is venerated, because she became the Mother, the cloud, the bridal chamber, and the ark of the Lord.

—Proclus of Constantinople,
Homily in *Mary and the Fathers of the Church*, 256

a very young age, that Mary was taught about her Jewish faith and then betrothed to an aged widower with children, Joseph. The picture we get of Mary from this book is one that emphasizes her ritual purity above all else.

The *Proto-Evangelium* was quite popular. Around 140 manuscripts of the book survive in its original Greek, as well as in several Oriental languages, including Syriac, and in Latin adaptations. The Eastern Orthodox view of James and the other figures in the gospels identified as Jesus' "brothers" (see Matthew 13:55; also Acts 1:14 and Galatians 1:19) derives from this text. They are identified as the widowed Joseph's children from his first marriage.

In general, for those who read it, the text was popular because it filled in gaps that still pique our curiosity today. Who were Mary's parents? How could she have even begun to be spiritually prepared for the amazing role God called her to?

The book is obviously a mishmash of various other texts, but because it is relatively early in its origin (and believe it or not, a hundred years after Jesus' life on earth is considered early), not all readers dismiss all of its claims so easily. Catholic devotional tradition certainly hasn't. Who knows what ancient memories it preserves, even as it embroiders on them?

The one element of the *Proto-Evangelium* that has had the most lasting impact on Christian devotion is the identification of Mary's parents as Joachim and Anne, and especially Anne as her mother. St. Anne is a very popular saint in her own right, and her role in Christian art is worth a brief detour because it gives us food for thought about her daughter as well.

One common image is what is called the "St. Anne Trinity." In this composition, Anne, Mary, and Jesus are pictured together, an arrangement that emphasizes the humanity of Jesus as rooted in his mother and grandmother. Another frequently found image is that of St. Anne doing what countless mothers through history have done: teaching her daughter to read. We see it first in the mid-thirteenth century, after which it became quite popular. This simple portrait of Anne and Mary, either sitting or standing and sharing a book, is seen in wall art, statues, stained glass, prayer books, and even primers for children.

In some cases, when he or she has room, the artist lets us see what's in the book placed between the women. It's often the text from Isaiah 7:14, which prophesied a king born to a girl, or virgin. Sometimes it is Psalm 45:11: "And the king will desire your beauty. . . ." When there's a lot of room, we might see *Domine labia mea aperies,* "O Lord, open my lips," which is the opening of Matins, morning prayer, in the Little Hours of the Virgin, a popular form of the Liturgy of the Hours commonly prayed by the laity.

The imagery here, as in all art, can be a rich source of contemplation. On a purely historical level, many scholars see the prevalence of the image as an indication of a period in which women were increasingly literate, and mothers, in particular, played an essential role in teaching their children, especially their daughters, how to read.

But spiritually there's more. What can we discern from this image of *Maria Lectrix,* "Mary the Reader," as it is called?

Perhaps for a moment we can ponder words. Or more precisely, the Word. In the first chapter of John, known as the Prologue, Jesus is described as the "Word" or *Logos* of God. The Word came to us through this young woman, taught to read by her mother. In Jesus, God speaks to the world. Jesus is the self-expression of the mind of God, just as the words you and I say express our thoughts. This Word is spoken in a language we can understand, the language of human beings whom God loved so much that he became one of them. One of us.

This Word—this savior, this redeemer—is not hidden or obtuse or only for the elite. His presence is not arbitrary or fleeting like that of the pagan gods. He is a gift, given to us to listen to, to hear, to respond to in love. All of us. All of us can hear this Word and respond.

Perhaps Anne taught Mary to read and understand not only words on a page or a scroll but the signs God would give her of what her child was about, who he would be for her, her people, and the entire world.

Taught to read the history of God's activity in the world, to know the names of the patriarchs and prophets, to recognize and sing the psalms, Mary was steeped in the word, so that when the time came, the Word would dwell within her. Then in the fullness of time, she could read that Word, respond, and teach us, in turn.

Mary's Daily Life

Nazareth was a village in Galilee, the northern part of Palestine, near, not surprisingly, the Sea of Galilee. The area was rural and, by our standards, poor.

Most scholars would say that Nazareth was composed of a few dozen families who lived in small homes of rock and mud, many of them built as extension of caves, with the caves used as storerooms. Recent excavations in ancient Nazareth (now a city of about sixty thousand people) have revealed tools and structures for processing olives and grapes.

Daily life for Mary would have been about work, just as it was for everyone else: working in vineyards or groves, doing craft work, cooking, caring for children. Joseph, a woodworker, would have been engaged in constructing some support structures for buildings—rafters and such—but was probably busiest with objects like tables and benches.

Politically, the region was under the control of the Roman Empire and had been for decades. Jewish leaders, on behalf of the empire, ruled locally. Galilee was governed by Herod Antipas, the son of Herod the Great. Herod Antipas is the same Herod before whom Jesus appeared on trial. Although taxation was heavy, life as a whole was fairly peaceful in Galilee during this period.

We don't have an exact picture of the daily spiritual life of Jews outside of Jerusalem. The center of spiritual life would have been the home, although, as we can see from the gospels, synagogues did exist. They were, however, centers for learning, not worship. Their role as places of worship wouldn't develop until after the destruction of the Temple in Jerusalem in A.D. 70.

Daily life would have been marked with prayer rooted in the psalms and other hymns we find in the Old Testament—for example, the hymn that Mary's namesake, Miriam, prophetess and Moses' sister, sang in praise of God for Israel's victory over the chariots of Pharaoh (Exodus 15:1-12). The various times of the day were marked with prayer, and certain days of the week might have been set aside for fasting. Those who could traveled the fifty miles to Jerusalem for important feasts that required sacrifice at the Temple.

Whether Mary, as the *Proto-Evangelium* says, grew up in the Temple or lived her young life entirely in Galilee, we can discern from her response to the angel Gabriel that she was deeply rooted in her Jewish faith, its trust in the God of Israel, and the promise of the Messiah, as the canticle Luke attributes to her, the *Magnificat,* shows.

And so we are back asking, who was Mary?

Our Lady of Loreto

The Holy House of Loreto, Italy, is a small structure of rocks surrounded by an enormous basilica and is honored as the Holy Family's Nazareth home.

How did it come to Italy?

Legends say it was flown by angels, but the truth is possibly even more interesting. The site in Nazareth had been honored from the early centuries, the original small home built over with churches and eventually buried as Muslims wrecked those same churches. Records indicate that in the thirteenth century, the building made its way to Italy due to the efforts of members of the Angeli family. They rescued the home from destruction by Muslim invaders and had it shipped back to Italy. Examinations of the stones of the Holy House reveal techniques and markings common in first-century Palestine.

Our Lady of Loreto is the patroness of air travelers.

THE IMMACULATE CONCEPTION

The immaculate conception is the ancient Christian belief that God preserved Mary from original sin from the time of her conception. The angel greeted Mary as being "full of grace" (Luke 1:28), which we understand to mean that God had filled her with the fullness of his grace so that she might be prepared for her great role in salvation history. In Mary's life, we see the powerful grace of God at work from the very beginning:

> The "splendor of an entirely unique holiness" by which Mary is "enriched from the first instant of her conception" comes wholly from Christ: she is "redeemed, in a more exalted fashion, by reason of the merits of her Son." The Father blessed Mary more than any other created person "in Christ with every spiritual blessing in the heavenly places" and chose her "in Christ before the foundation of the world, to be holy and blameless before him in love."
>
> —*Catechism of the Catholic Church, 492*

A young Jewish woman who lived an ordinary life of work and prayer, who lived in a spirit of gratitude to God and trust in God's power to save: a young woman who embodied the faith of the people of Israel.

In the midst of her work and prayer, that promise is fulfilled and Hope is born. In the ordinary life of Mary, the extraordinary takes shape.

Looking at Mary

In a culture transfixed by celebrity, in which mass communication makes it possible for any and all of us to publish our thoughts and transmit our images to potentially the whole world, in which personal worth is measured in terms of professional success and achievement, it is good every day to look at Mary.

It is astonishing, really, and something we'll come back to again and again. When you're out and about someday, find a young mother who may serve as a type of Mary for you—the youngest mother you can find in the congregation at church, at the mall, at the park. Watch this young woman, sitting in this particular spot on the earth, one of billions of human beings, smoothing her baby's back, murmuring in its ear, searching for a bottle, retrieving a toy, and when the baby is calm, leaning back and gazing at whatever it is in front of her, thinking, watching, and maybe even praying. Or perhaps she is pregnant, and when she leans back, she props her feet up, and her hand rests carefully on her belly, tapping, smoothing, massaging.

Into the life of a young woman like that—busy, thoughtful, worried, joyful—a young person who makes no laws and wields no power, God moved.

God moves and acts in whatever way he likes. Most of the time, what he seems to like is the small, the unexpected, the quiet, the ignored, those that the world cannot imagine could ever do anything of value.

Nothing has changed in two thousand years. This was the way God worked in Mary's life—and the way he works in ours. In our small spot on this earth, in the midst of our ordinary lives, God moves. God calls. God invites.

The Akathist Hymn

Devotion to the Blessed Virgin Mary has its origins in the East. Long before Marian devotion flowered in European or Western Christianity, Christians from Egypt to Asia Minor (now Turkey) were singing hymns to Mary, praying to her, and depicting her in icons.

One of the most ancient hymns to Mary is the *Akathist* hymn, probably written around the end of the fifth century and still in use in Eastern Catholic and Orthodox churches today. It has a particular place of honor on the fifth Saturday of Lent, which is called "Akathist Saturday."

The title of the hymn means "not seated," indicating that those singing or listening do so standing (the typical posture for Eastern Christian prayer). It is, like many of the psalms, an acrostic. Each of the twenty-four stanzas begins with successive letters of the Greek alphabet. As is the case with Eastern Christian prayer, the chant is a responsive one between priest, cantor, and people. The essence of it is a celebration of the mystery of the incarnation, Jesus the Son of God and Son of the Virgin. The first two chants, any single line of which could be a rich beginning of prayer and meditation, follow.[1]

First Chant

[Priest]: An Archangel was sent from heaven to greet the Mother of God, and as he saw you assuming a body at the sound of his bodiless voice, O Lord, he stood rapt in amazement and cried out to her in these words:

Hail, O you, through whom Joy will shine forth!

Hail, O you, through whom the curse will disappear!

Hail, O Restoration of the Fallen Adam!

Hail, O Redemption of the Tears of Eve!

Hail, O Peak above the reach of human thought!

Hail, O Depth even beyond the sight of angels!

Hail, O you who have become a Kingly Throne!

Hail, O you who carry Him Who Carries All!

Hail, O Star who manifest the Sun!

Hail, O Womb of the Divine Incarnation!

Hail, O you through whom creation is renewed!

Hail, O you through whom the Creator becomes
     a Babe!

Hail, O Bride and Maiden ever-pure!

[Response]: Hail, O Bride and Maiden ever-pure!

[Kontakion (Priest or Cantor)]:

Knowing that she was a virgin, the blessed one courageously answered the angel: "Your surprising words seem hard for my mind to accept: how can you speak of a birth that is to come from a conception without seed? And why do you cry, Alleluia?"

[Response]: Alleluia!

Second Chant

[Priest]: Trying to grasp the meaning of this mystery, the Virgin asked the holy messenger: "How is it possible that a son be born from a virginal womb? Tell me." And he answered her with awe, crying out in these words:

Hail, O hidden Sense of the Ineffable Plan!

Hail, O Belief in Silence That Must Be!

Hail, O Forecast of the Marvels of Christ!

Hail, O Fountainhead of truths concerning Him!

Hail, Celestial Ladder, by whom God came down!

Hail, O Bridge leading earthly ones to heaven!

Hail, O Wonder, ever-thrilling to the angels!

Hail, O Wound, ever-hurting to the demons!

Hail, O you who gave birth to Light ineffably!

Hail, O you who told no one how it was done!

Hail, O you who surpass the wisdom of the wise!

Hail, O you who enlighten faithful minds!

Hail, O Bride and Maiden ever-pure!

[Response]: Hail, O Bride and Maiden ever-pure!

[Kontakion (Priest or Cantor)]:

When the power of the Most High overshadowed the one who had never known the nuptial bed, her fruitful womb conceived, and she became for all a delicious field: for those who wished to reap salvation by singing "Alleluia!"

[Response]: Alleluia!

CHAPTER 2

The Annunciation

Familiarity with the story may have softened the impact, as it often does. These stories we have heard from childhood, these scenes that are etched in our consciousness lose their power to shake us. We think we know it all, we think that we understand the message, and we can move on.

But can we?

Should we?

Look at it again, this scene of the girl and the angel that Luke tells. Then glance back a few verses at what precedes it, the story of the priest and the angel. Is all of that just by way of prelude? Or should we stop for just a few minutes more before we turn the page?

Two Births

Luke begins his gospel with narratives of two birth announcements and then two births, both unexpected, both miraculous.

God seems to like working this way. Sara and Isaac. Hannah and Samuel. Samson and his unnamed mother. Skeptics sometimes suggest that this template is surely too neat, that all of these stories are simply constructed in imitation of each other—authorial variations on a theme. But might there be another way to look at it all?

What speaks to us more clearly about the meaning and promise of life than the birth of a baby? What assures us of the reality of love, what inspires us to wonder about the uniqueness and miracle of human life and its source more than the arrival of a child? What calls us to attend to the sacrificial, self-denying nature of real love more than a new life?

How can it surprise us, then, that God works powerfully in that small, miraculous place of one child's birth? We know that he does, for when we look at a newborn baby, we see something else, too. Something unique, not of our making, a destiny and hope that we could never have constructed even with the most sophisticated science. It makes sense and is, in fact, yet another sign of God's love for us that he works regularly and powerfully through the birth of a baby, building on the miracle, promise, and hope that we already sense in the barely open, squinting eyes.

Into this gathering of women—Sarah, Hannah, and Samuel's mother—enter two more: Elizabeth and Mary. Elizabeth, elderly and childless; Mary, young, unmarried, and childless. God will move in the lives of both in surprising ways.

But as similar as they are, there are differences in their stories, too, and it's in these differences that we see the first glimmer of just how radical a thing God is doing in the life of the girl from Galilee.

Elizabeth's husband, Zechariah, was a priest. Like all ordinary priests who were members of the tribe of Levi, he had a role to play in Temple life, offering sacrifice once a year. As we meet Zechariah, he is in the midst of fulfilling his responsibility in the inner recesses of the Holy of Holies, the chamber in which human beings could encounter God. But not all human beings—no women, no Gentiles, no non-Levites, no one who was ritually unclean could enter. Very few could actually go through that door into that Presence.

It was here, in this sacred space, that Zechariah receives the astonishing news that his elderly wife will become pregnant with a long-prayed-for child. Doubting, he is struck mute. The angel leaves. The angel has more work to do, more messages to deliver.

But the scene now could not be more different. We are far away from Jerusalem, in the small village that was never even mentioned once in the Hebrew Scriptures. We are not in a shrine or temple or synagogue. We are in the home of a girl no one has ever heard of, a girl who would never even be able to glimpse the door of the Holy of Holies, much less enter it.

And the angel has news for her, too:

In the sixth month the angel Gabriel was sent by God to a town in Galilee called Nazareth, to a virgin engaged to a man whose name was Joseph, of the house of David. The virgin's name was Mary. And he came to her and said, "Greetings, favored one! The Lord is with you." But she was much perplexed by his words and pondered what sort of greeting this might be. The angel said to her, "Do not be afraid, Mary, for you have found favor with God. And now, you will conceive in your womb and bear a son, and you will name him Jesus." (Luke 1:26-31)

It is well worth sitting with this for a while. Nothing, it appears, restricts God. Not biology, nor social expectation, nor religious institutions constrain him. God does as he will, and here he wills to break through the walls, come to his people, dwell in his own creation, as a zygote embedded in the womb of this anonymous girl.

Rejoice, indeed.

The Angel's Words

The first word that Gabriel addresses to Mary is most commonly translated as "greetings" or "hail." The most accurate translation would be closer to the English word "rejoice."

This word means something more than simply, "Be happy!" One of the things that really helps us read the Scriptures more fruitfully is to know that this word of God in human words, written across cultures and time, doesn't just speak to us—it speaks to itself. That is, there are themes and images that appear over and over, that are expanded upon, that take on new resonance during the long, rich history of God's people.

So as we listen to the angel, we're not just listening to a few words spoken at one moment. The angel's language is rich with allusions to Israel's past history and future hopes, a language (and this is important) that Mary would understand.

Even this single word, "rejoice," speaks volumes. We hear it several times in the prophets—in Zephaniah 3:14, Joel 2:21-27—as well as here, in Zechariah 9:9-10:

> Rejoice greatly, O daughter Zion!
>   Shout aloud, O daughter Jerusalem!
> Lo, your king comes to you;
>   triumphant and victorious is he,
>   humble . . .
>   and he shall command peace to the nations.

So when Gabriel greets Mary with, "Rejoice!" it's clear that something is up here, something that is not just about Mary but is about God's people, something that connects the present with the promises God has made for the future. Pope Benedict XVI, writing when he was Cardinal Joseph Ratzinger, said,

The greeting marks the beginning of the Gospel in the strict sense; its first word is "joy," the new joy that comes from God and breaks through the world's ancient and interminable sadness. Mary is not merely greeted in some vague or indifferent way; that God greets her and, in her, greets expectant Israel and all of humanity is an invitation to rejoice from the innermost depth of our being.[2]

The angel continues to greet Mary as "O favored one, the Lord is with you" or in our more familiar translation, "full of grace." Catholics have traditionally understood these words as expressive of Mary's immaculate conception—that as preparation for her role as mother of the Savior, God saved her from sin from the first moment of her existence.

There is a broader meaning as well. After all, what is grace? It is the life-giving presence of God. It is God's love, for God is love. To be "full of grace" is to be totally present to God, to be available to God for whatever God calls us to.

As the angel's words reveal, this is who Mary is. But she is not who she is for her own sake but for a greater reason: God's reason.

He will be great, and will be called the Son of the Most High, and the Lord God will give to him the throne of his ancestor David. He will reign over the house of Jacob for ever, and of his kingdom there will be no end.
(Luke 1:32-33)

The long, painful wait for a savior was to end. Mary would conceive the child of whom the prophets had spoken. The titles that the angel recites would have been familiar to Mary, for they had been in the hearts and on the lips of the people of Israel for centuries: the Messiah, the Anointed One, who would inherit the throne of Israel's greatest king and would reign at God's right hand.

Mary, understandably, is confused.

She objects that she is unmarried, that she does not "know man," is not sexually active. At this point, Mary is betrothed to Joseph, a more committed state than engagement, but still before a couple has lived together. The angel explains—sort of. But as is the case with all Scripture, what is explained is what we need to know. Not biology, not chemistry, but God.

What will God do?

Mary said to the angel, "How can this be, since I am a virgin?" The angel said to her,

> "The Holy Spirit will come upon you, and the power of the Most High will overshadow you; therefore the child to be born will be holy; he will be called Son of God. And now, your relative Elizabeth in her old age has also conceived a son; and this is the sixth month for her who was said to be barren. For nothing will be impossible with God."
> (Luke 1:34-37)

Even as Mary takes her place with this gathering of women of faith, she's now set apart in a radical way. All of these women had husbands and conceived their children in the human way. The angel reveals that something even beyond those miracles is happening with Mary.

Just like everything else the angel has said, this description of the Spirit overshadowing Mary is deeply evocative of other things God has done.

The Holy Spirit is expressive of God's creativity. In Genesis, it's God's spirit that "swept over the the face of the waters" before it all began (1:2). God's presence in clouds is also a familiar image. In Exodus a cloud covers the meeting tent holding the ark of the covenant, filling it with the "glory of the LORD" (40:35). When Jesus takes Peter, James, and John up on the mountain, a cloud surrounds them and the Father's voice is heard from the cloud (Mark 9:7).

The other women—Sarah, Hannah, Samuel's mother, and Elizabeth—have borne the fruit of God's answering their prayers. Mary is all of that and more. Within her, God is creating, moving, speaking, and dwelling. The Holy of Holies, the ark. Within her it is all recapitulated and evoked, not in buildings or mountains, but in a Person.

What She Says. What We Say.

Fiat.

Yes. Let it be done. God's will be done.

That's what Mary says.

What do we say?

The annunciation is one of the most popular subjects for Christian art. We find it depicted very early—a second- or third-century fresco in the catacomb of St. Priscilla is the most ancient—and what remains sets the template for almost every depiction in the next two thousand years: a young woman, seated, receiving the news from an angel.

While the subject remains consistent, unique elements of style come and go through the centuries. In Eastern iconic imagery from the ancient world to the present day, Mary has a royal aspect about her. She sits on a throne-like chair in an indeterminate location while the angel moves toward her. In medieval art, the location often shifts to a home. The angel holds a white lily, which is a symbol of Mary's purity. A dove hovers. Mary, more often than not, is seen being interrupted in the middle of her prayers, an open book on her lap or in her hand, a verse written in for us to contemplate. Perhaps Isaiah 7:14: "A virgin shall. . . ."

But what remains a constant is that central image of a young woman receiving startling, life-changing news.

And saying *fiat*.

Why does this image resonate so much with us? Is it simply because it is a lovely sentimental scene?

I don't think so. Of course we are awed by the moment, by what it tells us about Mary herself, as we honor her as God's handmaid.

But the moment holds more for us as well. When we see Mary, hear the angel's words, and then listen to her response, what do we hear in our own lives?

We hear the same good news that Mary heard—that God comes to save us and dwells in our midst, right here and now. Holiness—living in the joy of God's love—is given to all of us who approach God in all the places we live, places no one has ever heard of.

But God has.

What truly good news this is! Unlike the Jews in Mary's day, we need no longer peer into the inner recesses of the Temple, wondering what might be there. But we certainly are still tempted to believe that this life with God isn't for us or must be amazingly complicated and hard to navigate. After all, look at all the books on the spiritual life that are produced every year! Look at the programs that promise to reveal secrets and truth, the messiahs who try to capture our attention from television and billboards.

MARY'S PRAYER

As a handmaid, I submit to the Lord's orders; as clay, I entrust myself to the hands of the Potter; let the Craftsman realize his design in me, according to his authoritative will; let him miraculously bring about the extraordinary pregnancy in me, in conformity with his love for men. Let it happen to me according to your word; let your words be fulfilled in me, and let what happens be made completely manifest and true.

—Pseudo-Chrysostom, "On the Annunciation to the Mother of God," in *Mary and the Fathers of the Church*, 280

MOTHER, TEACH US

So we can turn to her in grave humility and say to her, "Look, you are one of us. Teach us the height to which we can rise. We can't bear Christ, but we can be pregnant with love for every human being, men and women alike in giving life to other people. Mother, teach us how to do it. Teach us how to love. Teach us how to hope. Teach us how to say 'yes' to the impossible."

—Catherine de Hueck Doherty,
"A Woman Wrapped in Silence"

A Hymn on the Nativity

A wonder is Your mother: the Lord entered her
and became a servant; he entered able to speak
and he became silent in her; he entered thundering
and his voice grew silent; he entered Shepherd of all;
a lamb he became in her; he emerged bleating. . . .

He entered, a mighty warrior, and put on fear
inside her womb. He entered, Nourisher of all,
and he acquired hunger. He entered, the One
who gives drink to all,
and he acquired thirst. Stripped and laid bare,
He emerged from [her womb], the One who clothes all.

   —St. Ephrem the Syrian, "Hymns on the Nativity," in
    Mary and the Fathers of the Church, 118–119

When we see Mary, we know the truth. God doesn't work in a complicated way. He comes to us: here, now, where we are.

When we see Mary, we see the total unpredictability of God; and since we've had that same experience of God's surprises in our own lives too, we feel the need to pay attention.

People often wonder how to know what God is telling them—how to discern God's direction. Mary tells us, and every other faithful friend of God tells us that the way to know God's will is to embrace a radical openness, to expect the unexpected. You have a better chance of understanding God's will if you accept the simple, fundamental reality that God's ways are not our ways.

Are we open to that possibility?

Another part of discernment involves simply being familiar with God's voice. It's like getting a call from an old friend. If we've not spoken in a while, we won't recognize her voice. If we don't know what's been going on in her life for the past twenty years, we'll find it hard to grasp what she's telling us until we've caught up.

The news Mary heard was new, but she was able to understand it to the extent that she did because she was immersed in the story of her people. This news wasn't just about her and her personal relationship with God. It was—and is—cosmic.

Perhaps our discernment might benefit from watching Mary and the angel. What is my discernment about, anyway? Is it about me and my personal sense of happiness and well-being, or is it about God's love and glorious plan for all his creation and the role, small but important, I might play in it?

Which brings us to the final light that the *fiat* casts on Mary and on us.

God is God, and that means that God can do whatever he wants, however he wants. But for some reason that has driven philosophers mad with the illogic and implications of it all, God has chosen to involve us in that doing. His creation, this world he makes, hurtles around the sun, dynamic and growing . . . and we are involved. We say yes, we say no, we say maybe. We are free, and in that freedom we are involved with God's work and God's ways.

We watch this young girl receive the news that God will reach down and embrace this world and make it new through her. Through her *fiat,* her yes.

Mary's yes changed her life.

What of ours? ❧

ve aria

Ave María, grátia plena, Dóminus tecum. Benedícta tu in muliéribus, et benedíctus fructus ventris tui, Jesus.

Sancta María, Mater Dei, ora pro nobis peccatóribus, nunc et in hora mortis nostrae. Amen.

Hail Mary, full of grace, the Lord is with thee; blessed art thou among women, and blessed is the fruit of thy womb, Jesus.

Holy Mary, Mother of God, pray for us sinners, now and at the hour of our death. Amen.

Why do we pray?

For so many reasons. We pray in our need; we pray to express gratitude and joy; we pray, hoping to help others in our prayer.

Weaving all of those reasons together is the primal sense that we are not alone. We are here, not because of a cosmic accident, but because we were put here by Someone who had a reason to do so. Someone who cares, who loves, and to whom we are still connected.

Praying is as natural as greeting anyone we love. It is as deeply rooted and unconscious as a baby's reaching out a chubby little hand to a friendly face in the middle of the night, as joyfully unthinking as the rush to embrace a friend or lover.

The most powerful, enduring, popular prayers are never planned, not imposed from above.

People just start praying them.

So it was with praying to Mary.

We find prayers directed to Mary quite early in Christianity. Not everywhere, not always, but here and there. The third-century *Sub Tuum*, which forms the frontispiece of this book, is one. So is an early prayer—the offertory for the fourth Sunday of Advent, the liturgies attributed to St. Gregory the Great in the late sixth or early seventh century.[3] But it was in the eleventh century that devotion to Mary really took off, as people started consciously combining the angel's and Elizabeth's greetings to Mary in a single expression.

This combining first seemed to have happened in what is called the "Little Office of the Virgin Mary." The office or, as we call it today, the Liturgy of the Hours, is the several-times-daily prayer organized around the psalms that religious men and women pray.

Through history, variations of the office have appeared, including many specifically for the laity, who wanted in some way to join in the monastic prayer. The Little Office, which included psalms that seemed to particularly evoke Mary, as well as other readings, originated in monasteries but soon became very popular with laypeople. A part of this office was the angelic and Elizabethan greetings.

So logical did the pairing of the greetings seem that it became a popular prayer itself and was referred to as "the

Ave." We have countless stories of medieval saints praying their Aves, often in sets of hundreds or even thousands. One fifteenth-century spiritual writer created a way of praying Aves that included a different scene from the life of Jesus with each recital of the greeting:

> Blessed is the fruit of thy womb, Jesus Christ, whom John baptized in the Jordan, indicating him with his finger as the Lamb of God.
>
> Blessed is the fruit of thy womb, Jesus Christ, whose feet Mary Magdalene washed with her tears and wiped with her hair, kissed, and anointed.
>
> Blessed is the fruit of thy womb, Jesus Christ, who, having gathered together his disciples, preached the kingdom of heaven to the world; who restored sight to the blind, healed the lepers, cured the paralytic, freed those oppressed by the devil.[4]

Eventually, a petition was added to the pair of greetings from Scripture, and the prayer we now call the Hail Mary was placed in the Roman Breviary in 1568. The Rosary as we now know it was included in the breviary in 1571.

The Hail Mary became part of our devotional life, not because anyone on high told the peasants and the craftspeople and the mothers and fathers and children to say it, but because they wanted to. Because they, like the angel and like Elizabeth, wanted to greet Mary: the mother of Jesus, the mother of "God with us," the mother of their Lord.

CHAPTER 3

The Visitation

In those days Mary set out and went with haste to a Judean town in the hill country, where she entered the house of Zechariah and greeted Elizabeth. When Elizabeth heard Mary's greeting, the child leaped in her womb. And Elizabeth was filled with the Holy Spirit and exclaimed with a loud cry, "Blessed are you among women, and blessed is the fruit of your womb. And why has this happened to me, that the mother of my Lord comes to me? For as soon as I heard the sound of your greeting, the child in my womb leaped for joy. And blessed is she who believed that there would be a fulfillment of what was spoken to her by the Lord."

—Luke 1:39-45

Why was Mary in such a hurry?

Was it to hide her pregnancy from the people of Nazareth for as long as possible? Was it because the journey would be a relatively long one?

Practical questions intrigue us, but in the end, they don't answer the real question because it isn't a pragmatic one. It's spiritual.

Why did Mary set out "with haste"?

Because she had received *good news*—the best of news. In addition to her own pregnancy, the angel had also told her of Elizabeth's pregnancy. God was acting in these women's lives in startling, wondrous, and mysterious ways.

Who wouldn't be in a hurry to talk about it?

A Family Greeting

When Mary sets out, the angel has told her that Elizabeth is in her sixth month of pregnancy. Elizabeth and Zechariah's home was about seventy miles from Nazareth at Ain Karim, a village a bit west of Jerusalem that has been traditionally remembered as "the Judean town in the hill country." We don't know how she traveled. By foot, mostly, perhaps partway on a donkey or a cart. Horses were only for the military and the aristocracy. Depending on how she traveled, it might have taken Mary up to a week to reach Ain Karim.

Let's try to put ourselves in Mary's place. We can remember great news we have received. A clean bill of health. A college acceptance. A pregnancy. A birth.

For most of us, our first instinct is to share such good news. We grab the phone, we dash off e-mails, we make a surprise appearance at work. And who's receiving the news?

Those who love us, but more specifically, those whom we trust will understand and rejoice with us because they love us and because they have been in that joyful place, too.

And so, Mary traveled "in haste."

In just a few verses, we're immersed in this rather complex dance between Mary and Elizabeth. Mary comes to Elizabeth because of what the angel has told her, and Elizabeth understands because of what was revealed to Zechariah. For Elizabeth knew that her son would "make ready a people prepared for the Lord" (Luke 1:17) and that he would be a prophet.

When Mary's voice echoes through Elizabeth's flesh to reach John, he knows. He leaps because he knows, and here, for the first time, John bears witness to the Messiah.

How interesting that the first person to recognize Jesus is an unborn child.

Ain Karim

Scattered sources from the sixth century onward attest to the association of Ain Karim with the family of John the Baptist. A seventh-century writer notes a village festival in honor of Elizabeth; however, any early physical artifacts were obliterated by Arab presence in the early Middle Ages. In the fourteenth century, Crusaders brought a more substantial Christian presence to the area, and in subsequent centuries, various shrines and churches were built and religious communities settled there—most notably the Franciscans, who are well known for their care of religious sites in the Holy Land.[5]

Today pilgrims to Ain Karim visit the Church of St. John the Baptist, the Sanctuary of the Visitation, and "Mary's Spring," where Mary's meeting with Elizabeth is remembered.

The feast of the Visitation, first celebrated by Franciscans in the thirteen century, was extended to the whole Church in the fourteenth century. It's now celebrated on May 31.

MARY, THE ARK OF THE COVENANT

Many readers of Luke have noticed a parallel between Elizabeth's greeting to Mary and David's approach to the ark of the covenant. The ark, as you recall, was the structure built to house the tablets of the Ten Commandments. Its presence was experienced as the very presence of God, and when it was lost to enemies—which it was at times—Israel was weakened and even defeated.

At one point, King David goes to retrieve the ark, but realizes his (and Israel's) unworthiness, saying, "How can the ark of the LORD come into my care?" As he later accompanies the ark into Jerusalem with celebration, he speaks of being blessed by the presence of the ark (2 Samuel 6:9-14).

As is always the case, Christians pondered this and saw the hand of God throughout all of Jewish and Christian tradition, weaving meaning and revelation. In Elizabeth's greeting to Mary, they heard echoes of David's cry and, naturally enough, saw a new ark, bearing a new manifestation of God's protective, loving, powerful presence: Mary, the new ark of the new covenant.

Blessed Are You

At the sight of Mary, Elizabeth rejoices. She calls Mary "blessed . . . among women." Such praise has been offered to women before in Jewish tradition. Deborah, a judge of Israel, says it of Jael (see Judges 5:24), and Judith was called "blessed . . . above all other women on earth" (Judith 13:18). Both of these women played decisive roles in defeating Israel's enemies, and so will Mary because of the fruit of her womb, the Messiah, or as Elizabeth says explicitly, "My Lord."

Elizabeth's words reflect not a sophisticated, advanced understanding of Jesus' divine nature, but an awareness of the uniqueness of this child—related to God so closely that he could be called "my Lord," the same "Lord" for whom Zechariah had been told John would ready the world.

As time passed, Christians developed the need to explain Jesus' divine nature to a bigger, more philosophically conversant world always ready to diminish that divine nature. So they reflected on Elizabeth's words to Mary and heard something. Taken in the context of the rest of the gospels, in which Jesus' intimacy with and identity with God the Father was revealed, they saw it as evidence of Jesus' divinity and agreed, in the midst of the usual complicated theological disputes, that it was quite right to refer to Mary as *Theotokos*, "God-Bearer" or "Mother of God."

Here, as is the case with all the titles we give to Mary, the ultimate point is not about Mary but about Jesus. As we clarify who Mary is, we are really clarifying who Jesus is. This explains, too, why thinking about Mary is so important for Christians. She grounds our thoughts. When we are tempted to see our faith as one simply of ideas and concepts, to remember Jesus in the most general terms, we are, over and over, confronted with Mary. We have to bring ourselves back and remember: Jesus had a *mother*. He grew to life within her, he was born, he matured in her care.

Then the contemplation takes another turn, as we remember the good news of who Jesus is, the one the angel called *Emmanuel*, which means "God with us." In the moment when the pregnant Mary meets the pregnant Elizabeth and the baby John leaps within his mother's womb, we see something important about God. As an ancient prayer says, "He whom the entire universe could not contain was contained within your womb, O *Theotokos*."

For centuries, the disciples of Jesus have easily and joyfully incorporated Mary into their spiritual lives. With the angel, we greet Mary. With Elizabeth, we call her blessed.

Why? Because we sense that in greeting Mary, we welcome the Christ she bears.

In greeting her, we offer indirect but powerful praise to God, for it is God who has done this. God has entered creation in this most ordinary moment, in this most ordinary way.

In the meeting of Mary and Elizabeth, so much resonates and gently gestates outside the women's wombs. Mary has traveled so far, in haste, to meet the older woman whom, we are told, had been living in seclusion herself.

One travels, one welcomes, and in their meeting, in this visitation, we see the heart of hospitality, welcome, and friendship.

One way to look at it is this: these two women recognize the action of God in each other's lives. They have listened and heard good news about each other, and they bring it all into their encounter. They treasure each other. They treasure the new lives growing within. They are attentive to those little lives as well.

All because they listened . . . and welcomed.

Throughout the Scriptures, the simple act of hospitality is highlighted for us again and again. For ancient peoples, hos-

The Quickening of St. John the Baptist

Her salutation
Sings in the stone valley like a Charterhouse bell:
And the unborn saint John
Wakes in his mother's body,
Bounds with the echoes of discovery.
Sing in your cell, small anchorite!
How did you see her in the eyeless dark?
What secret syllable
Woke your young faith to the mad truth
That an unborn baby could be washed in the Spirit of God?
Oh burning joy!
What seas of life were planted by that voice!
With what new sense
Did your wise heart receive her Sacrament,
And know her cloistered Christ?

   —Thomas Merton, "The Quickening of St. John the Baptist,"
            in *The Collected Poems of Thomas Merton,* 200

pitality and welcome were sacred obligations, for as Abraham learned, you never know who it is who has come to call (see Genesis 18:1-10).

Jesus makes it clear who comes to call, though. Every time. Whatever you do to the least of these, you do to me (see Matthew 25:40).

That couldn't be clearer than it is in this encounter, this visitation. It is Jesus, come to call in the womb of the woman blessed to carry him. Elizabeth knew this because she listened to what the angel had told her husband; she knew because she was attentive to her own son, awakened with the start of recognition within her body.

Mary rushed to Elizabeth because she had listened to the angel. She knew that Elizabeth was old and pregnant—how difficult that must be! She knew that Elizabeth's pregnancy was the work of God and was related to the miracle growing within her. She listened, she pondered, as Luke tells us, and she responded.

ON THE DEVOTIONAL SIDE

The Angelus

What do we do to mark the passing of the day?

We listen for familiar sounds. We eat. We go to work or school or finally, home. We practice our instruments, we read newspapers, we do some gardening, we feed the baby, we take our walk.

And perhaps, like scores of our brothers and sisters in this Christian family, past and present, we pray.

Praying to mark the hours of the day is an almost universal practice, not confined to Christianity. In fact, the Christian habit of praying the psalms at various times of the day is rooted in Jewish practice.

One of the most familiar if not exactly ancient ways of marking time for Christians is what is called the Angelus. As the name implies, this devotion has something to do with angels, specifically the angel Gabriel, who greeted Mary with the news of the annunciation.

The development of this devotion is sketchy but seems to have begun in the early Middle Ages with the practice of reciting the *Ave Maria* three times at the ringing of an evening bell, coinciding with the end of Compline, the last prayer of the Daily Office, or Liturgy of the Hours.

Praying in the morning seems to have followed, and by the sixteenth century, we see the devotion more or less as we have it today, with prayers recited at morning, noon, and night, every day of the year except during the Easter season when a different devotion, called *Regina Coeli,* or "Queen of Heaven," replaces it.

V. The Angel of the Lord declared unto Mary.
R. And she conceived of the Holy Spirit.
Hail Mary, etc.

V. Behold the handmaid of the Lord.
R. Be it done unto me according to thy word.
Hail Mary, etc.

V. And the Word was made Flesh.
R. And dwelt among us.
Hail Mary, etc.

V. Pray for us, O holy Mother of God.
R. That we may be made worthy of the promises
    of Christ.

Let Us Pray:
Pour forth, we beseech Thee, O Lord, Thy grace into our hearts, that we to whom the Incarnation of Christ Thy Son was made known by the message of an angel, may by His Passion and Cross be brought to the glory of His Resurrection. Through the same Christ Our Lord. Amen.

Our busy lives are so focused on the things of this world. Even during the course of just a morning, our spirits can deflate, our hope falter. Praying the Angelus, even by ourselves as we eat lunch at our desk, sit in traffic, or fold yet one more load of laundry, might just have the power to open our hearts to the reality that amid the ordinariness, God lives, God invites, God dwells, and that perhaps our yes, like Mary's, can change so much.

CHAPTER 4

The Magnificat

For Mary, life has changed. You might even say it's turned upside down. Elizabeth's world is a bit different too, weighted by an unexpected, unlikely, growing baby boy. In that small village in the hill country of Judah, the two women met, embraced, shared their good news, marveled, and wondered what it all could mean.

Then, like faithful women everywhere, past and present, they praised God.

And Mary said,
"My soul magnifies the Lord,
    and my spirit rejoices in God my Savior,
for he has looked with favor on the lowliness of his
       servant.
    Surely, from now on all generations will call me blessed;
for the Mighty One has done great things for me,
    and holy is his name.
His mercy is for those who fear him
    from generation to generation.
He has shown strength with his arm;
    he has scattered the proud in the thoughts of their
       hearts.
He has brought down the powerful from their thrones,
    and lifted up the lowly;
he has filled the hungry with good things,
    and sent the rich away empty.

He has helped his servant Israel,
in remembrance of his mercy,
according to the promise he made to our ancestors,
to Abraham and to his descendants for ever."
(Luke 1:46-55)

When I think about anxiety and stress in my own life, it strikes me that the root of much of it is a sort of battle. Negativity and darkness come from a place where I'm dissatisfied, not accepting of things as they are, even fighting what my conscience tells me is true. Perhaps that's been the case in your life, too, and perhaps you know something else: when you relax and say yes, a burden lifts and almost naturally, you feel a shift deep within—a shift that opens your eyes to grace.

After all, what has happened to Mary and Elizabeth could be seen as, if not terrible news, then disruptive, dangerous, and potentially burdensome news. But instead of saying, "What if . . ." or "If only . . ." or "I wish . . . ," Mary sings out, "Thank you!"

What a difference that makes.

The Canticle

This song of praise, or canticle, is one of three in the first two chapters of Luke. Mary's is the first, followed in a few verses by one prayed by Zechariah after the birth of John (John 1:67-80), and finally by Simeon's briefer canticle in the Temple (Luke 2:29-32). (Simeon's canticle, known as the *Nunc Dimittis*, is prayed every evening at Compline, the last prayer of the day in the Liturgy of the Hours.)

Mary's canticle is popularly known as the *Magnificat* because that is the first word of the Latin translation of the first line: *Magnificat, anima mea, Dominum*, "My soul magnifies the Lord."

If you are familiar with the songs of praise that course through the Hebrew Scriptures, the *Magnificat* will certainly sound familiar. In Mary's words, we hear reverberations of the psalms, we hear the hope of the prophets, and we even hear echoes of another woman given the gift of a child by God. Her name was Hannah, and after fervent prayer and vows to God, she became pregnant and bore her own son, Samuel, who was to be the last judge of Israel and the prophet who would anoint the first two kings, Saul and David. Her canticle, found in the first book of Samuel, resounds with the same themes as Mary's: gratitude to God for all he has done, especially his victory over the wicked, his care for the poor and the lowly, as well as an understanding of the world in which God shakes the powerful and raises up the poor:

> Hannah prayed and said,
> "My heart exults in the LORD;
> my strength is exalted in my God.
> My mouth derides my enemies,
> because I rejoice in my victory.
>
> "There is no Holy One like the LORD,
> no one besides you;
> there is no Rock like our God.
> Talk no more so very proudly,
> let not arrogance come from your mouth;
> for the LORD is a God of knowledge,
> and by him actions are weighed.
> The bows of the mighty are broken,
> but the feeble gird on strength.
> Those who were full have hired themselves out for bread,
> but those who were hungry are fat with spoil.

The barren has borne seven,
   but she who has many children is forlorn.
The LORD kills and brings to life;
   he brings down to Sheol and raises up.
The LORD makes poor and makes rich;
   he brings low, he also exalts.
He raises up the poor from the dust;
   he lifts the needy from the ash heap,
to make them sit with princes
   and inherit a seat of honor.
For the pillars of the earth are the LORD's,
   and on them he has set the world.

"He will guard the feet of his faithful ones,
   but the wicked shall be cut off in darkness;
   for not by might does one prevail.
The LORD! His adversaries shall be shattered;
   the Most High will thunder in heaven.
The LORD will judge the ends of the earth;
   he will give strength to his king,
and exalt the power of his anointed." (1 Samuel 2:1-10)

Many modern scholars are of the opinion that Luke has not actually quoted Mary in this canticle but constructed it by adapting a song of praise familiar to the community, or even simply by adapting Hannah's song of praise to fit the narrative.

Perhaps. Or perhaps not. With all due respect to Scripture scholars and the important, enlightening work that they do, it's important to remember one thing: they change their minds. They disagree. Theories that were all the rage two decades ago lie in the dustbin today, some forgotten and some held up ruefully as the new generation of scholars wonders, "How could anyone have ever believed that?"

More important, many Scripture scholars are just like the rest of us: they have their opinions as to what is and isn't possible, what could and couldn't be true. You can examine the same text with different presuppositions and emerge with completely different conclusions.

So it is with the *Magnificat*. Many come to the text convinced of the impossibility of Mary's composing such a canticle and then remembering it.

Is it really so impossible?

After all, the gospels make clear that Mary was a thoughtful person. She wondered. She pondered. She held things in her heart. There is nothing in the gospels to indicate that she was ignorant or uninvolved in her religious traditions. There's also nothing in Luke's text that implies she came up with this canticle right there, on the spot. She'd had time to ponder what the angel had told her, time on the journey to experience the subtle but real signs of early pregnancy. She had traveled from Nazareth to Jerusalem, traversing the terrain of the Holy Land, the land promised by God to Abraham, drawing closer every day to Jerusalem, the holy city, the festal city, the city in which God's presence was keenly and powerfully felt.

She traveled this way, contemplating the words of the angel that she had been overshadowed by the Most High, whose presence was worshipped in the Temple, feeling, trusting the presence within her, remembering the prayers she had heard sung and chanted her whole life, including perhaps, even Hannah's song.

Suddenly the idea that this song of praise to God might indeed be Mary's, borne of her heart and memory, remembered and treasured for years to come, doesn't seem quite so absurd.

Pope Benedict XVI put it more broadly:

> The *Magnificat*—a portrait, so to speak, of her soul—is entirely woven from threads of Holy Scripture, threads drawn from the Word of God. Here we see how completely at home Mary is with the Word of God, with ease she moves in and out of it. She speaks and thinks with the Word of God; the Word of God becomes her word, and her word issues from the Word of God. Here we see how her thoughts are attuned to the thoughts of God, how her will is one with the will of God. Since Mary is completely imbued with the Word of God, she is able to become the Mother of the Word Incarnate.[6]

My Soul Magnifies the Lord

Being with Elizabeth inspires Mary. All of these things she'd been mulling over, the amazing news she'd received come together at last through Elizabeth's response to her. The same is often the case with us. Our news—good or bad—takes on another shade of meaning when it's affirmed by the presence of someone who shares that experience. What we've been thinking about can't be contained any longer; and so, like Mary in the presence of her once-barren cousin with a baby leaping in her womb, as David leaping before the ark on the way to Jerusalem, we exult.

When we are part of something astonishing and new, we know that we're in the middle of something bigger than ourselves, something miraculous and true, and this is what Mary expresses. We can almost hear the words tumbling out of her in that way of chanting and singing so typical of ancient prayer. In her soul, in what is happening to her, in her small, humble self, God is magnified. He looms large and powerful because the promise is finally being fulfilled.

What promise?

The ancient promise of redemption: of healing of a broken world; of mercy flowing; of the poor, those who know that their lives depend on God, being rewarded; and the haughty, proud, and rich, who think they need nothing except their own powers, being sent away.

The world, damaged by sin so that it values power and domination, is saved and set right by the small, the unnoticed, and even the despised. Mary, in awe that she's a part of this, praises God.

Of course!

Our Praise

Mary's *Magnificat* might help us think about our own prayer lives.

What is that like? What is it like for you to pray? What does God hear on his end of things?

Jesus tells us over and over to bring all of our needs to God. No matter how small our request, no matter how small we think of ourselves, like the widow coming before the judge, the neighbor needing help in the middle of the night, Jesus tells us to bring him all, whenever we feel so moved and however often we need.

But he also gave us a commandment. A first commandment. A greatest commandment: to love the Lord your God with all your heart.

What is love if it is not expressed? In our prayers of praise and gratitude, we live in obedience to the greatest commandment. After all, how authentic would we judge the affection of another from whom we only heard requests and needs?

A CHILDBEARING VIRGIN

Gabriel pronounces; Christ is received into the Virgin's body.
The womb swells because of the holy Offspring.
We are exhorted to believe in something new,
And never seen before:
A childbearing Virgin.

—Hilary of Poitiers, "Hymn on Christ," in
Mary and the Fathers of the Church, 188

To praise, to thank, to bless. This is at the heart of prayer. If you look at traditional Jewish and Christian prayer, you will find some very interesting and perhaps startling things. You'll find that traditionally, Jews and Christians throughout history haven't conceptualized prayer primarily as "making stuff up in your head and spilling it out to God."

No, when the ancient spiritual writers thought and wrote about prayer, they were thinking first of all of praise—of what we as creatures owe the Creator every day. Both Jews and, following in their stead, Christians divided the day into hours marked by prayer that were always sung, chanted, or spoken aloud, and that were overwhelmingly prayers of praise. All of creation grew, moved, and breathed in gratitude for its existence, and we join in the song.

Look carefully at Mary's prayer. For what is she praising God? Satisfying her needs, making her personally "happy," or fixing her problems?

Not really. It seems as if she is praising and thanking God for his power and his mercy and that she, his handmaid, is playing a role in his plan of redemption, of shaking the world out of its self-satisfaction and self-reliance, turning that world radically, like the poor, back to dependence on God.

Mary sings that her soul "magnifies" the Lord. In the words of Joseph Ratzinger, to magnify the Lord means

> not to want to magnify ourselves, our own name, our own ego; not to spread ourselves and take up more space, but to give him room so that he may be more present in the world. It means to become more truly what we are: not a self-enclosed monad that displays nothing but itself, but

God's image. It means to get free of the dust and soot that obscures and begrimes the transparency of the image and to become truly human by pointing exclusively to him.[7]

Our spiritual lives, our lives with God, really are journeys. Like Mary, we travel along the road, trying to piece it all together. We've not yet reached our destination. Our prayer reflects that when it is small, self-referential, anxious, crabby, and resentful that life is not going according to our plan and that the world is not making us happy.

Mary's prayer teaches us another way. It points to the destination: a joyful spirit that understands, no matter how small we seem, that God has put us here for a reason. In that fact and in our efforts to let God love the world in our daily choices and encounters, God is magnified. In the midst of the cosmic drama of passionate love, our hearts are joined to Mary, and we praise.

The Rosary

If there's any object, aside from a crucifix, that identifies a Catholic, it's a rosary. They rattle in pockets, tangle up in purses, clatter against pews, and swing from car mirrors.

Like everything else in Catholic spiritual life, the Rosary as a devotional prayer grew organically from the practices of ordinary people, without a straight line of development. In the early Middle Ages, laypeople all over Europe sought to join their prayer to those living in monasteries. The center of monastic prayer is 150 psalms, traditionally prayed over the course of one week. In imitation of this prayer, the habit of praying 150 *Pater Nosters* (Our Fathers) or *Ave Marias* (Hail Marys) developed. (The street in London in which rosary makers were concentrated is still called Paternoster Row.)

Over time, beads were used as a way of counting, and the prayers were divided into sets. During the fourteenth and fifteenth centuries, roses came to be associated with Mary, and prayers and a sets of prayers centered on her was thought of as a rose garland, or *rosarium*.

During this period, the spiritual practice of meditating on scenes from the gospels while praying the beads grew in diffuse and diverse ways. The whole devotion was formalized in the sixteenth century, and the feast of the Most Holy Rosary was established on October 5 in commemoration of the role of the Rosary in defeating the Muslim invading forces at the Battle of Lepanto in October 1571.

The formalization of the Rosary involved the three sets of mysteries that traditionally comprised the devotion:

The Joyful Mysteries
The Annunciation
The Visitation
The Nativity
The Presentation
The Finding in the Temple

The Sorrowful Mysteries
The Agony in the Garden
The Scourging at the Pillar
The Crowning with Thorns
The Carrying of the Cross
The Crucifixion

The Glorious Mysteries
The Resurrection
The Ascension
The Descent of the Holy Spirit
The Assumption
The Crowning of Mary as Queen of Heaven

In 2002 Pope John Paul II issued an apostolic letter, *Rosarium Virginis Mariae,* "The Rosary of the Virgin Mary," in which he added a new set of mysteries: the Luminous Mysteries. They are so called because they focus on the ministry of Jesus and the light that came into the world because of it.

The Luminous Mysteries
   The Baptism of the Lord
   The Wedding Feast at Cana
   The Preaching of the Kingdom of God
   The Transfiguration of the Lord
   The Institution of the Eucharist

People pray the Rosary for many different reasons. Common to all of them, though, is the sense that through praying this Mary-centered prayer, we come closer to Jesus. The concreteness of these beads as they slip through our fingers is a vivid reminder of the concreteness of God's love, entering our lives, as we are, right here and now.

In his apostolic letter, Pope John Paul II says best how praying with Mary can help us draw closer to the reality of Jesus:

Mary lived with her eyes fixed on Christ, treasuring his every word: "She kept all these things, pondering them in her heart" (Luke 2:19; cf. 2:51). The memories of Jesus, impressed upon her heart, were always with her, leading her to reflect on the various moments of her life at her Son's side. In a way those memories were to be the "rosary" which she recited uninterruptedly throughout her earthly life.

Even now, amid the joyful songs of the heavenly Jerusalem, the reasons for her thanksgiving and praise remain unchanged. They inspire her maternal concern for the pilgrim Church, in which she continues to relate her personal account of the Gospel. Mary constantly sets before the faithful the "mysteries" of her Son, with the desire that the contemplation of those mysteries will release all their saving power. In the recitation of the Rosary, the Christian community enters into contact with the memories and the contemplative gaze of Mary.[8]

CHAPTER 5

Pregnancy and Birth

The gospels tell us nothing about Mary's pregnancy except for its very beginning and its end. But without straying into pious fantasy or fiction, and since nothing indicates that hers was in any way not a normal pregnancy, it's not inappropriate to meditate on the not-so-simple truth of the word-made-flesh growing among us. Growing in Mary's body, a body that changed like any woman's during pregnancy. Her breasts grew heavier, the first visible sign of pregnancy as the body prepares to nourish a child. A slight thickening, a bump, a bulge, and then a firm, strong, weighty place, a home for the child, forming in warm darkness.

Slowly, the baby makes himself known directly. He flutters at first, like shy butterflies inside you, movement so slight and unexpected you are never sure if it is you or him. It is hard to tell the difference, hard to separate it out.

Then there is a kick. A definite kick.

Finally, near the end, when you are so heavy and there is just the thinnest, ever-tightening layer of skin and muscle between the baby and the rest of the world, there is no doubt that someone is in there. Even an observer can see and might even be able to discern a knee, heel, or elbow. You can give him a little push so he'll back off your ribs. He might even push back.

Millimeters away, but in another world. Closer to you than anyone else could ever be, but still a mystery. So to fill in the blanks, you imagine. Sitting at your desk, lying in bed, standing at the well at Nazareth. You still yourself, and you feel the baby, who it seems has always been with you and some days feels like it always will be. It's hard to remember a time that he wasn't.

You wonder who he is. You might even make up little stories, imagine scenes of what he's doing in there, what he thinks when you are still, what he does when you move around, what he wonders when you eat something spicy (if you still can). You can almost hear him murmuring there in the waters, in the shrinking space within. Always, in your imaginings, he is wise. Wiser than any real baby could ever be, but still, the dancing, rolling, kicking babies we imagine within us always seem to be wise beyond their years.

Even after birth, in that early, blurred, squinty-eyed gaze, we see some of that wisdom. We watch them watch us and listen to them listen to us, calmly, blinking rarely, staring. What are they listening to? The music of the spheres? We see them stare at the ceiling, and we look, too. What do they see that we, our gaze narrowed by life in the world, can't? Angels? Sometimes I wonder.

So as Mary grew, Jesus grew within Mary. They settled into life with Joseph, patiently waiting in the midst of villagers, some of whom minded their own business, others who did not.

Mary had at least a few clues about her son. She knew he was a boy. She knew that he was from God, promised to save Israel. But still questions had to remain, questions we're told Mary pondered and wondered about and searched through and, we can assume, prayed about. Perhaps she prayed the psalms, and even her own canticle, over and over again, waking every morning, remembering with a start what the angel had said, and relaxing, resting in the prayer of praise.

We've seen already that Mary's role as the mother of Jesus is about more than one woman's relationship to her child. When we contemplate this reality of the Creator God moving in the womb of a woman, what we are contemplating is the incarnation itself. God meets humanity in the body of a woman. When we watch Mary, when we contemplate what God is doing in her life, we watch all of humanity being embraced by God, indwelt and clothed.

That is why we honor Mary. That is why a Christianity that seeks to drive Mary away is deficient and actually makes the gospel less clear. Mary is us. She is our part of the relationship. She stands for us in the mystery.

Mary longs to see her child, like any pregnant woman, wanting to know the one who dwells within her. Each person—indeed, humanity itself—longs, as well. We long for the fulfillment of our own deepest desires for life, for unconditional love, for joy that never ends, for healing. In Mary's longing for the Promised One within we see our own longing. With Mary, we yearn for the promise to be fulfilled. And we patiently wait, trusting, letting God do his work, letting God's presence grow within us, letting him be magnified.

The spiritual writer Caryll Houselander wrote beautifully about what all this means in her classic, *The Reed of God*:

If Christ is formed in our lives, it means that He will suffer in us. Or, more truly, we will suffer in Him.

"And He was made man."

Our Lady saw at once what was meant in her case: supernaturally, He was made herself.

If He is made man in you, he will be made you; in me, me.

It is extremely difficult to lay hold of this fact. It is very hard not to think of a kind of mystical Christ just beside us, or just in front of us, suffering with infinite patience and joy, being obedient, humble, persevering, fulfilling His Father's will.

It is really difficult to realize that if He is formed in our life we are not beside Him but in Him; and what He asks of us is to realize that it is actually in what we do that He wants to act and suffer.[9]

A Child Is Born

At last, the time came. But not in the expected way (as if anything could be expected in these circumstances). And not in the easy way. Instead of birthing at home, in a familiar place with women she knew and trusted, Mary first had to make a journey.

We find the narratives of Jesus' birth in the gospels of Matthew and Luke. While they both relate the same fundamentals that Jesus was born in Bethlehem and was virginally conceived, the accounts differ from that point on.

These differences have been explained in various ways, ranging from the conclusion that the stories were simply fabricated by the evangelists to fit the general themes of the gospels to the assumption that the various aspects of the stories are rooted in the perspective of different witnesses—particularly Joseph for Matthew, and Mary for Luke.

We really don't know the answer. What we do know is that the gospels, while written as testimonies of faith, were also written out of the assumption that they were telling the truth:

Since many have undertaken to set down an orderly account of the events that have been fulfilled among us, just as they were handed on to us by those who from the beginning were eyewitnesses and servants of the word, I

THE DEFENSELESSNESS OF GOD

In the child Jesus, the defenselessness of God is apparent. God comes without weapons, because he does not wish to conquer from outside but desires to win and transform us from within. If anything can conquer man's vainglory, his violence, his greed, it is the vulnerability of a child. God assumed this vulnerability in order to conquer us and lead us to himself.

— Cardinal Joseph Ratzinger,
Images of Hope: Meditations on Major Feasts, 12

MASTERS AND SERVANTS

Whoever is poor should be consoled by this: Joseph and Mary, the Mother of the Lord, had neither servant nor handmaid. They came to Bethlehem by themselves from Nazareth. They did not have a pack horse. They are masters and servants at the same time. This is new!

—St. Jerome, "Homily on the Nativity of the Lord," in
Mary and the Fathers of the Church, 213

THE VIRGIN IN SOLITUDE

The Virgin, harboring a mystery under her heart, remains in profound solitude. In a silence that almost causes the perplexed Joseph to despair. Incarnation of God means condescension, abasement, and because we are sinners, humiliations. . . . Those whose lives God enters, those who enter into his, are not protected. They have to go along into a suspicion and ambiguity they cannot talk their way out of. And the ambiguity will only get worse, until, at the cross, the Mother will get to see what her Yes has caused and will have to hear the vitriolic ridicule to which the Son is forced to listen.

—Hans Urs von Balthasar, "Conceived by the Holy Spirit, Born of the Virgin Mary," in *Mary: The Church at the Source*, 155–156 too decided, after investigating everything carefully from the very first, to write an orderly account for you, most excellent Theophilus, so that you may know the truth concerning the things about which you have been instructed. (Luke 1:1-4)

It should also be obvious that since the four canonical gospels evolved only decades after Jesus' life on earth and since there was no attempt to harmonize Matthew's and Luke's accounts, perhaps the memory of Jesus' origins, preserved in his family and then shared, included all the elements we find in both Matthew and Luke. Each evangelist highlighted the aspects of the account that most powerfully illustrated his own inspired account of Jesus.

So in Matthew, who emphasizes Jesus' fulfillment of Jewish prophecy even more than the other evangelists, we find copious references to the Hebrew Scriptures. Matthew's gospel also emphasizes Jesus' mission to the Gentiles—to the whole world. Consider, for example, how the gospel ends, as Jesus tells his apostles to go out and "make disciples of all nations" (28:19). In his infancy narrative, Matthew emphasizes just this point—we see the end of the gospel encapsulated in the beginning. In fact the entire gospel is compressed into those first two chapters, as Herod the Great, the King of the Jews, hears the news of Jesus' birth, rejects him, and seeks his death. It is the Gentiles—the Magi from the East—who recognize Jesus and honor him.

On the other hand, Luke's gospel offers us a special emphasis, not only on Mary but on the poor as well as on forgiveness (Luke 11 is a chapter full of parables of mercy). Luke highlights the announcement of Jesus' birth to shepherds, not the visit of the Magi. According to the Jewish law, shepherds were in a bad way because they were more or less perpetually ritually unclean, since they were constantly dealing with blood and corpses as they tended to the life cycles of their flocks.

So just as earlier in Luke, we see the marvelous fact of God's breaking through the Temple walls to touch the world through the life of an unknown girl from an unknown place, after Jesus' birth, in a place of poverty, rejected by a world that had no room for him, the Good News bursts forth, not to the religious establishment or earthly powers—but to shepherds. The unclean. The lowly, waiting well outside the town walls, deep in the night.

Glory to God!

Listening with Mary

Since ancient people were directly in contact with the world day and night, in a way that we simply no longer are, they were alive to signs and portents coursing around them. We complain that God doesn't speak to us so clearly anymore, that there are no angels, no stirrings of the Spirit, no pointed dreams; but honestly, if there were, who would hear them? Who would see? Who would unplug their ear buds, turn down the volume, be still and just listen?

Mary did, of course. Once again, we look to her for the other half of this story of redemption. How do we respond?

John has no infancy narrative in his gospel. Instead, he reaches further back, to the preexistence of Jesus, long before time, before the earth. He begins his gospel by identifying Jesus as the Word. *Logos* is the Greek word, and it has many nuances. In this context, we can hear echoes of more than simple "logic." Jesus is the self-expression—the literal word of God. He also is expressive of the divine principle of reason and order, of the meaning that we can see in every aspect of creation, from the marvels of a cell to the expansiveness of the universe.

One of the most dangerous temptations of the Christian life is to get tied up in knots figuring out how to squeeze this amazing, rich, expressive, infinite Word into a baby.

How can the infinite reach for his mother's breast, cry, be taught to walk, tumble down laughing amid his squeals? How could this be?

Such twisting and turning misses the point. Think of words. What is our general attitude toward them? When we (if we're open-minded) hear words spoken to us, do we immediately try to impose meaning on the words and try to fit them into our reality?

Well, perhaps we do. But that leaves us no better off, no wiser than we were before.

However, we all know that to grow in wisdom and spirit, when confronted with a word, we listen.

We let the word speak to us. We ponder. We reflect.

So here he is, finally out of Mary's womb.

Her uterus has contracted and she has pushed and he has emerged, been cleaned, fed, wrapped up, and laid down to rest after such a short (but such a very long) journey.

The Lord sleeps. The Word rests, breathing softly in the cave that shelters animals. Shepherds nearby awaken to the signs.

What is God telling you about himself?

Listen. With Mary. Listen.

I think God is telling us all we need to know.

And so with Mary, we listen. We listen to the Word of Mercy, now laid in a wooden manger, whose life on earth would end in a passion of love laid out on a wooden cross.

It is God who has done this, but we come back to this point again and again: God has done this, given us exactly what our broken hearts and lives need and so deeply desire, by clothing himself in human flesh, by speaking our language, by touching us with hands through which our own blood rushes.

And this flesh—our flesh—is Mary's. As Houselander writes, she gives herself over to God, giving her flesh, and so God enters the world through us:

That is what it meant to Mary to give human nature
    to God.
He was invulnerable; He asked her for a body to be
    wounded.
He was God; He asked her to make Him man.
He asked for hands and feet to be nailed.
He asked for flesh to be scourged.
He asked for blood to be shed.
He asked for a heart to be broken.
The stable at Bethlehem was the first Calvary.
The wooden manger was the first Cross.
The swaddling bands were the first burial bands.
The Passion had begun.
Christ was Man.
    . . . A few words spoken to an angel and heard only by
him: "Be it done unto me according to they word."
    Then, like the pause that measures music as truly as
the sounds, the word of God is silent; for nine months it
is inaudible.
    It is the pause during which the opening phrase grows
within us in loveliness, preparing our minds for the coming
splendour.

Suddenly drifting down the darkness, like the bleat of a lamb, comes the cry of a newborn infant.

Now it is no longer Mary's voice uttering the word. Nevertheless it is her voice, for it is the human voice that she has given to God.[10] ⬎

ary's arden

The incarnation isn't just an idea. It's an astonishing reality that defines and shapes how we, disciples of this word-made-flesh, live in the world.

In faith that "God so loved the world," we meet God through bread and wine; we are joined to him by being washed in water and smeared with oil. We even identify ourselves quite literally as his body and aren't afraid to let the things God has created speak to us of his kindness and love directly or through the witness of other members of this body.

So, of course, when it comes to Mary, we have our icons and statues. We have our medals and pictures. And we also have our plants!

Mary's life appeals to us in part because it is so rooted in this world God has made—in pregnancy and birth, in the everydayness of a life that was shaped by the rhythms of nature, in the closeness to God's earth of a woman birthing a baby in a stable, with shepherds waiting nearby, listening. Jesus is described as sprouting from the root of Jesse's tree.

One of the ways people have expressed this connection to Mary, one of God's creatures chosen in the midst of life to bear the Savior, is to associate her with other living, growing, life-nurturing things. In fact, during the Middle Ages, it became popular to plant a "Mary Garden" filled with plants that reflected various aspects of Mary's life and, therefore, the graces and love showered on her by God.

The Mary Garden was also seen as a symbol of the Church that has grown, in a way, from Mary's yes and from the fruitfulness of her womb: alive, diverse, fruitful, beautiful, in service to God's great plan.

Roses: The pre-Christian association of roses with love and beauty was rather effortlessly adopted by Christians, who graced art and architecture with this representation of God's love for us and our love for God. Mary, in particular, was thought of in terms of roses, and often depicted holding roses. In Dante's *Divine Comedy*, Beatrice, Dante's guide through paradise, says to him: "Why are you so enamored of my face that you do not turn your gaze to the beautiful garden which blossoms under the radiance of Christ? There is the Rose in which the Divine word became flesh: here are the lilies whose perfume guides you in the right ways."[11] White roses traditionally represent Mary's purity; red, her sorrows; and gold, her glory in heaven.

Lilies: Artists often depicted Mary holding a white lily in annunciation scenes. A legend says that lilies filled Mary's tomb after she was assumed into heaven. In the eighth century, the English Church historian the venerable Bede wrote that the white petals of the lily represented the purity of Mary's body, and the golden antlers, the goodness of her soul.

Rosemary: Rosemary is a fragrant, needle-shaped herb that grows on bushes. A popular legend says that the plant received its scent as a reward from God after it provided a place for Mary to spread Jesus' newly washed clothes on the journey to Egypt.

Violets: These small, delicate flowers symbolize Mary's humility. Legend describes them blossoming as Mary responds to the angel's good news with her *fiat*.

Marigolds or "Mary's gold" represent her domesticity and simplicity. In the popular imagination, marigolds adorned her clothing.

Strawberries: Often used by artists in borders of paintings of Mary or under her feet, strawberries symbolize the "fruitful Virgin," as well as the glory of the souls in heaven.

That's only the beginning. Many more plants have been associated with Mary through the ages. They are living reminders of the life-giving love of God, brought to intimate, real life in Mary and the fruit of her womb.

Chapter 6

The Presentation

Bringing a new life into the world is an astonishing responsibility. How many new parents have looked down at their baby in the crib, then looked up at each other and wondered, "What have we done?"

This is why, through most of history, hardly any culture has left child rearing up to two hapless newborn parents alone. Grandparents, aunts, uncles, and friends join together in traditional societies to help provide support, structure, a common set of values, and many pairs of watchful eyes.

When confronted with the tiny new life of infinite potential, our religious sensibilities kick in as well; and naturally enough, we turn to God, not only in gratitude but in prayer for help and blessing.

Marking the beginnings of new life and new families is something all cultures and religions do in some way. As Luke takes pains to show us, Mary and her family plunged right into that river of wisdom and strength, fulfilling the obligations that all Jewish families embraced upon the birth of a child.

First, Luke notes, Jesus was circumcised (see Luke 2:21) at the traditional age of eight days, the age prescribed by God to Abraham (see Genesis 17:12). Circumcision was the sign of a boy's membership in the covenant between God and Israel, the point at which he was also named. During Jesus' time, which was some decades before the synagogue had really developed into a center for learning, a boy was usually circumcised at home by his own father.

Catholics have traditionally celebrated the feast of the Circumcision on January 1, eight days after December 25. On today's liturgical calendar, it is overshadowed by the celebration of Mary, Mother of God, but clearly the two are related as celebrations of Jesus' human nature.

After the circumcision, Luke describes yet another journey for Mary and Joseph and the baby—a journey to Jerusalem from either Nazareth or Bethlehem to the Temple.

> When the time came for their purification according to the law of Moses, they brought him up to Jerusalem to present him to the Lord (as it is written in the law of the Lord, "Every firstborn male shall be designated as holy to the Lord"), and they offered a sacrifice according to what is stated in the law of the Lord, "a pair of turtledoves or two young pigeons." (Luke 2:22-24)

Two things are apparently going on here, and whether Luke has confused the two rituals or is relying on a jumbled report is not known. We'll briefly tease them apart.

In addition to circumcision, two other birth-related rituals were prescribed for Jewish people during this period. First was the "presentation" of a child to the Temple. As Luke indicates, it is rooted in the tradition first described in Exodus 13 of consecrating or dedicating a firstborn child to the Lord for the Lord's service. The importance of the firstborn shouldn't be a surprise—many sacrifices called for the first fruits of a harvest or the firstborn animal. In faith we give God the first fruits of our labor, believing that he deserves the beauty of this new life in thanksgiving, and trusting that there will be more to follow for our own needs.

By Jesus' time, however, the ritual had changed a bit. An entire tribe of Israel was exclusively dedicated to the service of God in the Temple—the Levites—so it was no longer the practice for every family to literally give over the firstborn child to that service. The act was symbolic, and it was actually followed by a "buying back" of the child (five sheckels in the first century) for those not in the Levitical tribe. Animal sacrifice was, of course, still a part of Jewish practice and would be until the destruction of the Temple in A.D. 66, so that was a part of the ritual as well. The normal offering would be a newborn lamb, along with two turtledoves or two pigeons. The lamb could be dispensed with if the family was poor, and as we see from Luke's account, such was the case with Jesus' family.

But there's something else in those verses—a reference to "purification." Purification was a practice, also rooted in ancient Jewish tradition (see Leviticus 12), related to the ritual purity of women after childbirth.

Traditional Judaism had extensive and detailed purity laws. Scholars debate the origins and purpose of these laws, but all agree that the essence of them was to set God's people apart as holy—a living, breathing symbol of God's holy presence in the world.

Sometimes people confuse ritual impurity with sinfulness. This was not how the Jews of Jesus' time understood it at all. Ritual purity related to worship and the ability to enter into the presence of God through worship. One can only approach God if one is "clean" in the sense of being undefiled.

Aside from food concerns, a major area for Jewish ritual purity had to do with the body, and particularly contact with excretions, especially blood and running, open sores. Women were considered ritually unclean during and a few days after

CHURCHING OF WOMEN

"Churching" is a Christian ritual that combines a remembrance of Mary's purification with a prayer for women who have just birthed children. It seems to have begun during the Middle Ages. In the ritual, women come to church forty days after the birth of a child, often with a candle, and have prayers recited for and over them by the priest. It reflects a time in which women stayed at home—even in bed—for weeks after childbirth, a period called "laying-in." The ritual is a way of welcoming the new mother back into the church community. The rite was common in Latin Rite Roman Catholicism up until Vatican II and was part of the Anglican tradition as well. It is still frequently practiced in Orthodox and Eastern Catholic churches today.

THE PURIFICATION OF MARY

On this day, the entire populace of the city is gathered together as one, all aglow with the brilliant light of candles, and together celebrates Holy Masses. And no one may enter the public assembly who does not hold a lit candle in his hands, like one going to offer the Lord in the Temple and, indeed, about to receive him. And by the devotion of their outward offering, they show the light that is burning in their hearts. . . . Now [the Virgin] offers the Lord to the prophet of prophets; she offers the One to one man, but in offering him to one, she offers him to all, for she gave birth to the one Savior of all.

—Ambrose Autpert, "On the Purification of Holy Mary," in *Mary in the Middle Ages*, 44 their menstrual periods. For the same reason, they were considered ritually impure after childbirth.

Leviticus 12 says that in order for women to be clean again, they must undergo a purification: thirty-three days after the birth of a boy and sixty-six days after the birth of a girl.

At that point, the woman undergoes a ritual washing. This kind of ritual washing is still a part of Jewish life today, particularly among the Orthodox.

We can't say for sure what Mary would have done, but she may have undergone her ritual purification in the Temple. Perhaps the family did use the journey to Jerusalem to celebrate both Jesus' presentation and Mary's purification.

What Mary and Joseph were doing, Luke makes clear, is fulfilling their religious duties, participating in rituals that identified them as part of God's people, obeying God's laws, and affirming their participation in the covenant.

Religious obligations can so often seem like just that—obligations. Not surprising, since in Catholic practice, the commitment to attend Sunday Mass is actually called an "obligation."

Who hasn't experienced the consequences? Who hasn't struggled at times to see the point? Who hasn't chafed at requirements, suspected that spiritual growth might better be found in freedom from these obligations, wondered if doing it our own way on our time, creating our own rituals and relying on our own intuitions of when, where, and how to honor God would better serve us?

When those thoughts hit, it might be a good time to look at Mary.

Mary, graced with a more intimate knowledge of God than any of us could ever enjoy, carrying him within her own body for nine months, nursing him at her breast, reflecting for almost a year now on the words of an angel, didn't and couldn't see herself beyond all religious obligation. She did not and could not put herself above and beyond the wisdom and practices of God's people.

So she went to Jerusalem, presented her baby, presented herself, and offered sacrifice.

As we've said before, what Mary experienced was not just between her and God. In fact, the "her" at the heart of this wasn't just herself, Mary. She stands for all of us, the humanity to whom God reaches out and embraces, seeking to be embraced in turn.

In the *Magnificat*, Mary expresses gratitude not only for what God has done for her but also for the amazing, surprising twist in God's story of mercy and redemption for the whole world. So Mary doesn't stay by herself in the village, tending to her child, keeping him to herself. She immerses them both in their tradition, embracing the obligations because they are all a sign of God's love. These rituals are meeting places between God and his people, a place where now God steps again, in the arms of his mother.

Perhaps what we read and absorb in Luke can be an encouragement to us as we fulfill our own religious obligations. Perhaps it can help us view them more joyously, as chances to enter into the love song of God's people and their movement towards God, and be open to the surprises, revelations, and comfort that we might experience there if we approach with truly open hearts.

Encounters at the Temple

As Luke tells it, the Holy Family encounters two fascinating people at the Temple, two prophets, one male and one female:

Now there was a man in Jerusalem whose name was Simeon; this man was righteous and devout, looking forward to the consolation of Israel, and the Holy Spirit rested on him. It had been revealed to him by the Holy Spirit that he would not see death before he had seen the Lord's Messiah. Guided by the Spirit, Simeon came into the temple; and when the parents brought in the child Jesus, to do for him what was customary under the law, Simeon took him in his arms and praised God, saying,

"Master, now you are dismissing your servant in peace,
    according to your word;
for my eyes have seen your salvation,
    which you have prepared in the presence of all
        peoples,
a light for revelation to the Gentiles
    and for glory to your people Israel."

And the child's father and mother were amazed at what was being said about him. Then Simeon blessed them and said to his mother Mary, "This child is destined for the falling and the rising of many in Israel, and to be a sign that will be opposed so that the inner thoughts of many will be revealed—and a sword will pierce your own soul too."

There was also a prophet, Anna the daughter of Phanuel, of the tribe of Asher. She was of a great age, having lived with her husband seven years after her marriage, then as a widow to the age of eighty-four. She never left the temple but worshiped there with fasting and prayer night and day. At that moment she came, and began to praise God and to speak about the child to all who were looking for the redemption of Jerusalem. (Luke 2:25-38)

Simeon's prayer is called the *Nunc Dimittis* and is prayed every night at Compline, the last prayer of the Church's Liturgy of the Hours. Two things stand out to us from Simeon's prayer: the image of light and what he says to Mary.

Simeon holds the baby Jesus and describes him as a "light for revelation to the Gentiles." In these words, we can clearly hear Isaiah, prophesying hundreds of years before, comforting suffering Israel with the news that indeed a time would come when their pain would end and God would send them a redeemer who would—and this is important—be a light to the whole world, Gentiles and Jews alike (see Isaiah 9:1-3). Here, in the baby held in his arms, Simeon, a man of age and wisdom, discerns the light.

The Presentation of the Lord is a feast that is celebrated in the West on February 2 and is traditionally known as Candlemas. Inspired by Simeon's insight into Jesus' identity, Christians celebrate this day with candles; for centuries, a procession with candles was an integral part of the feast, and today, at the very least, a blessing of candles plays a role in the Mass.

Simeon's words to Mary, though, are startling. He speaks of the child as an occasion for division—traditionally translated in the well-known phrase, "a sign of contradiction." Many will follow, he says, but many will stand in opposition.

How true we know this to be!

And then, what of Mary?

Every mother, looking at her new baby, has high hopes and dreams for that baby. But at the same time, she has fears. She checks the baby during the night, watching his tiny chest rise and fall, listening for breathing sounds. She watches older children lurching toward trouble, and she prays. In her mind, she knows that no one can avoid pain and suffering, but she can't imagine anything happening to her own; she can't imagine what it would feel like to see her own child suffer.

It might just feel like a sword through her soul.

For what Simeon reveals here in his aged eyes, his trembling arms holding the quiet baby, is what they all know. Standing there in the river of Jewish tradition, there in the Temple, near the presence of the Most High, they know the fate of prophets. They know the continual suffering of God's people. Even though the hopes and expectations of a messiah are all about glory and victory, they remember, perhaps, the other image Isaiah describes, a figure chosen by God, one who serves, and one who suffers.

So Mary takes the baby back after the prophetess Anna has had her say, returning to ordinary life with this extraordinary child with even more to think about than before.

So much truth is revealed in the midst of these simple acts: God's light shines, here and now, through Jesus. After all, how much more clarity about God's love for us do we need beyond the reality of his presence among us as a helpless child?

Still more—the world, infected by sin, resents this light that shows sin and evil for what it is and that shines brightly, calling us to make a choice.

The way to the final, eternal banquet God seeks to lay out for all of creation is one of pain. Not because God wants it so, but because we know, through our own lives, that the more intensely the light of love shines, the more vigorously darkness resists.

This way to eternity lived in God's light, the light that shines forth from the baby's eyes, will hurt. And once again, this truth that we all know, that we all face, that we all struggle through is faced first by Mary.

MARIA LACTANS

A good way to see how Christians have understood the humanity of Jesus is to examine how artists have represented him. Not surprisingly, his relationship to his mother has provided much inspiration through the centuries, an affirmation of the conviction that one of the reasons that Mary is so important is that she stands as a constant reminder of his humanity.

One of the most powerful and spiritually evocative images in art is that of *Maria Lactans*—Mary breastfeeding Jesus. We find early examples in the catacombs of Rome, but the popularity of the image really reached its peak during the Middle Ages and the Renaissance. The image is symbolic on a number of levels. It reveals Jesus' humanity and humility, the reality of the incarnation, by linking Mary to the traditional way of representing the virtue of charity, which is an image of a nursing mother who gives of herself to give another person life. The symbolism also spills over into reflections on Jesus' relationship to us, as in St. Ephrem the Syrian's *Hymns on the Nativity*:

> Mary bore a mute Babe
> though in Him were hidden all our tongues.
> Joseph carried Him,
> yet hidden in Him was a silent nature older than everything.

The Lofty One became like a little child,
yet hidden in Him was a treasure of Wisdom that suffices
    for all.
He was lofty
but He sucked Mary's milk,
and from His blessings all creation sucks.
He is the Living Breast of living breath;
by His life the dead were suckled, and they revived.
Without the breath of air no one can live;
without the power of the Son no one can rise.
Upon the living breath of the One Who vivifies all
depend the living beings above and below.
As indeed He sucked Mary's milk,
He has given suck—life to the universe.[12]

The first Marian shrine in North America, established in the early seventeenth century in St. Augustine, Florida, is *Nuestra Señora de La Leche y Buen Parto,* "Our Nursing Mother of Happy Delivery."

ON THE DEVOTIONAL SIDE

Salve Regina

It's the last prayer of the day in the monastery. In the half-darkness, after the psalms have been chanted, the day pondered, and the night welcomed, there is time for one more prayer:

> Hail, holy Queen, Mother of Mercy,
> our life, our sweetness and our hope.
> To thee do we cry, poor banished children of Eve;
> to thee do we send up our sighs,
> mourning and weeping in this vale of tears.
> Turn then, most gracious advocate,
> thine eyes of mercy toward us;
> and after this our exile,
> show unto us the blessed fruit of thy womb, Jesus.
> O clement, O loving, O sweet Virgin Mary.

Then it is time to sleep.

The *Salve Regina,* "Hail Holy Queen," is a prayer of strong emotions, which is perhaps why it is so popular. Its origins are someone ambiguous, but the most probable account of its composition only deepens its emotional and spiritual resonance.

Tradition has it that the author of the *Salve Regina* was an eleventh-century monk named Hermann Contractus or, in less sensitive eras, Herman the Cripple. He had been left on the island monastery as a baby by his parents, who evidently decided that the monks could take better care of their severely disabled child than they could. Perhaps they were right, for Herman grew up, despite his nearly total immobility and difficulties in speech, to be a formidable intellect who composed histories, scientific compendiums, and mathematical theorems.

And hymns. He most certainly is the author of *Alma Redemptoris Mater*; and because of that and some documentary evidence, he is the strongest candidate for the composition of *Salve Regina*. When you put the prayer into the silence of an island-bound monastery and the seeking soul of a man abandoned by his own mother and constrained within an uncooperative body, both our sympathy and our hope can only grow.

Although at first glance, the prayer seems to stray away from proper devotion to Mary, a closer look shows that this is not the case. Mary is "Mother of Mercy" because she is mother of Jesus, who is mercy.

We ask only two things of Mary in this prayer: to listen to us and, in the end, to point us, at long last, to Jesus, in whom we can find rest. Perhaps part of the reason that this prayer became almost immediately popular as a before-sleep prayer is because, in a sense, it gives us what we almost intuitively hope for ourselves and what we remember from our own childhoods: that evening time when a sympathetic ear listens to the problems of the day, a gentle hand soothes our brow and assures us that all will be forgiven, all will be better, all will be healed—soon.

CHAPTER 7

The Finding of Jesus in the Temple

Lost and found. Seeking, finding, patience. Mysteries.

The curtain is drawn back on those "hidden years" of Jesus only once in the gospels. Luke tells the story, in a few verses at the end of the second chapter, before we jump ahead two decades to meet John the Baptist again, preaching at the Jordan River.

As is always the case with the Scriptures, and one of the reasons we keep coming back to it throughout our lives, the story of the finding of Jesus in the Temple is on one level our own story, one that every person can identify with: a child edging beyond his parents' understanding, the fear of losing a child, the relief of finding, the general mystery of not quite understanding each other.

In Mary's actions we see our own searching for something precious, panicked with fear that it might be lost forever. In her words, we hear our own confusion and frustration at the mysterious doings of other people, even people we thought we knew. And as she listens to Jesus speak to her, we listen, too.

For the third time in these opening chapters of Luke, we are in the Temple in Jerusalem. This section of Luke, called the "infancy narratives," begins and ends in the Temple. Stepping back and taking an even broader view, we see that in fact the entire Gospel of Luke begins and ends in the Temple. From Zechariah before the birth of John to the disciples after the ascension, returning to the Temple in Jerusalem where they were "continually . . . blessing God" (Luke 24:53), Luke helps us understand Jesus as the fulfillment of God's promises to his people through their history and tradition.

Luke reports that Jesus and his family had journeyed to Jerusalem from Nazareth with a larger pilgrimage group because it was the feast of Passover. Before we get to the meat of this story, it's good to note that this journey is actually the same journey that Jesus' public ministry takes, as well: from Nazareth to Jerusalem—to the cross—at Passover time (Luke 9:51–19:28).

The Temple, God's presence, God's wisdom, a journey. Jerusalem as a destination, as a place where things are revealed to those who will listen. A mother, a disciple, us.

Now we can listen to the story as it is, as well as for its greater resonance within the whole story that Luke tells us about Jesus:

Now every year his parents went to Jerusalem for the festival of the Passover. And when he was twelve years old, they went up as usual for the festival. When the festival was ended and they started to return, the boy Jesus stayed behind in Jerusalem, but his parents did not know it. Assuming that he was in the group of travelers, they went a day's journey. Then they started to look for him among their relatives and friends. When they did not find him, they returned to Jerusalem to search for him. After three days they found him in the temple, sitting among the teachers, listening to them and asking them questions. And all who heard him were amazed at his understanding and his answers. When his parents saw him they were astonished; and his mother said to him, "Child, why have you treated us like this? Look, your father and I have been searching for you in great anxiety." He said to them, "Why were you searching for me? Did you not know that I must be in my Father's house?" But they did not understand what he said to them. Then he went down with them and came to Nazareth, and was obedient to them. His mother treasured all these things in her heart.

And Jesus increased in wisdom and in years, and in divine and human favor. (Luke 2:41-52)

By this point in Jewish history, the spring religious celebration had extended to eight days: Passover with the Seder meal on one evening and the Feast of Unleavened Bread continuing for seven days afterward (Leviticus 23:5-6). The spring celebration was one of three pilgrimage feasts during which male Jews were obligated to celebrate in Jerusalem. The others were the Feast of Weeks (Pentecost) and the Feast of Tabernacles.

We don't know how widely this law was observed, but many people did make the journey, swelling the population of Jerusalem with Jews, not only from Palestine but also from the Diaspora, speaking many languages, as the first chapter of Acts describes quite vividly.

At this time, a boy was considered a male responsible for fulfilling religious obligations when he turned thirteen, although this is more than a millennium before the formal ritual of *bar mitzvah* was instituted. A boy of twelve, as Luke very specifically describes Jesus as being, was in between. He was certainly welcomed and encouraged to participate as much as he could as a way of formation, but he was generally free to take his place with either the men or the women and children, who in this culture were strictly segregated according to gender. The sexes did not intermingle in worship or in general social interaction either, except with members of their own family—a necessary bit of

FAITH SIMPLIFIES THE SEARCH

Where must we seek?
Everywhere—in everyone.
How must we seek?
With faith and courage and limitless love.
First of all, by faith. . . .

Faith simplifies the search. We do not have to discover in which of several people Christ is to be found: we must look for Him in them all. And not in an experimental spirit, to discover whether He is in them or not, but with the absolute certainty that He is.

—Caryll Houselander, *The Reed of God*, 98, 103

A SPACE TO ABIDE

Mary "puts together," "holds together"—she fits the single details into the whole picture, compares and considers them, and then preserves them. The word becomes seed in good soil. She does not snatch at it, hold it locked in an immediate, superficial grasp, and then forget it. Rather, the outward event finds in her heart a space to abide and, in this way, gradually to unveil its depth, without any blurring of its once-only contours.

—Cardinal Joseph Ratzinger, "'Hail, Full of Grace': Elements of
Marian Piety according to the Bible," in
Mary: The Church at the Source, 71

background, incidentally, for grasping the full force of Jesus' interaction with women during his ministry and the place of women among his disciples (see Luke 8:1-3).

So that's the scene. A large group, most related in some way, traveling the three or four days from Nazareth to Jerusalem for the feast. A "full day's journey" was about twenty miles. They arrive, celebrate the Passover, part of which involves obtaining a lamb that has been sacrificed in the Temple, roasting and eating it, and keeping all bones unbroken in the process. During the Seder meal, they remember and celebrate God's great act of power and mercy in freeing the Israelites from slavery in Egypt.

After this, the family might stay for as long as it liked in Jerusalem or simply head home.

One family started home, a busy caravan full of mothers and fathers, aunts, uncles, cousins, and grandparents. One day out, two parents, Mary and Joseph, settled in for the night and naturally enough started looking for their son, Jesus. He was nowhere to be found.

A twenty-mile walk back to Jerusalem followed. You can imagine the fears, not to speak of other feelings. How could he have been lost? How could he ever be found? You don't have to be a parent to identify.

On the third day of searching, Luke tells us, he was found. He was in the Temple, conversing with the elders, the teachers, both listening and talking to them. He was in the midst, we might imagine, of that heady river of rabbinic exploration and learning, of close examination of the text, which continues today.

But as Luke notes, there was something unusual—indeed extraordinary—about this boy, who had not yet reached the age of maturity, conversing with the elders. They were astounded. *Existanai* is the Greek word used, a word Luke uses eleven times, more than any other evangelist. As the angel told Mary, as the angels sang to the shepherds, someone extraordinary is here.

You can imagine the combination of relief, confusion, and perhaps a little aggravation that the family felt. Mary gives voice to these feelings when she asks, "Child, why have you treated us like this? Look, your father and I have been searching for you in great anxiety."

Luke doesn't describe Mary's tone, but perhaps we can hear in her words, if not quite anger at least frustration and confusion. Almost as if she was saying, "You've never given us reason to worry before!" It is as if this act, perceived in simple human terms, was a surprising departure from Jesus' usual way of obedience and respect. The word she uses, *odynasthai*, alludes to mental and spiritual pain. This has torn at her, it seems.

God's Promises

We've compared Mary to Abraham before, and perhaps this tiny moment gives another example. Abraham, asked to sacrifice his son Isaac, is tested not only on the level of human connection, but also on the level of understanding God's promise. Isaac was a child of promise, the one from whom the descendants of Abraham, as numerous as the sand on the shore and the stars in the sky, would come. Without him, how could God's promise be fulfilled?

Perhaps Mary has been puzzled, even tormented, by a similar question in those three days she searched for and wondered about her son. This, too, was a son of promise—of great, specific, glorious promise—given twelve years ago by an angel, confirmed by the prophet in her cousin's womb. His name Jesus was given at the direction of God himself through an angel. Emmanuel. God with us. How could he be gone? What of God's promise now?

But Jesus makes clear then that this is just something Mary will have to get used to. As Mary has alluded to "your father," Jesus asserts that another relationship takes precedence: "Why were you searching for me? Did you not know that I must be in my Father's house?" (Luke 2:49).

These are the first words that Jesus speaks in Luke's gospel. They confirm who he is and what he is about. Right here, in the Temple, Jesus makes clear not only his own identity, revealing who he is, but, by implication, especially when we listen to him in the context of the rest of the gospel, something about where a disciple's ties lie. Luke is very keen for us to understand what discipleship means. There are many dimensions to discipleship, the central one being just that: who is at the center? A disciple is a student, any disciple of Jesus faces these central questions: "Are you really Jesus' disciple and his alone? Are there other voices to which you listen, other loyalties that divert you from the way? Whose lessons are you learning?"

This book is about Mary, and what we have focused on time and time again is what Mary teaches us about being a disciple. Here, it seems, the hard part of the lesson is really beginning, a clear example of the sword that Simeon prophesied was in her future.

This is the part about discerning loyalties, about choosing your master, about experiencing the tension between heaven and earth. Even as the story is worked out right here on earth, amid family ties, we are challenged to look beyond them.

We will see this again. In between now and the cross, the only interactions that Jesus has with his mother in the gospels bear an almost dismissive tone. It is not disrespectful, for as Luke takes pains to point out, the young Jesus returns with his parents to

Nazareth, obediently. But there is also a clarity about what Jesus says to and about his family, including his mother, as well as family ties in general (see Luke 14:26; 12:51-53).

What Jesus says to Mary here in the Temple is first of all about his identity and his vocation. God is his Father, and God's business is his vocation. It's an identity that the angel revealed to Mary when she was told Jesus would be "the Son of the Most High," and the identity is further confirmed in the chapter following this during Jesus' baptism (Luke 3:22).

If we didn't know the rest of the story, Jesus' words would end there, with his own identity. But since we know what happens later, on another journey from Nazareth to Jerusalem, and we know who Jesus gathers along the way, what he tells them, and what he calls them to, we hear his words of singular identity and commitment, and we as his disciples find our direction as well.

Who am I listening to? Who am I learning from? From the world and its cacophony of exploitative, false voices? Or from the Son of the Father, a baby, a boy, a man on the cross, calling me to follow, promising the truth of eternal life?

Whose business am I about?

Mary hears this, and we don't know exactly how much she understood. Luke says that "they," which might include just the teachers or his family, including Mary, didn't understand. Luke tells us that Mary "treasured" these things in her heart, something that immediately reminds us of her response to the shepherd's presence at her baby's birth. Taken together, we have a sense of what it means to be wise, to be contemplative, meditating on what God has done in our lives, because Mary leads the way.

Sometimes nonbelievers like to accuse Christians of taking some sort of comfortable way out, a life full of easy answers. In saying that, they make clear that they've never talked to any actual Christians, for any disciple of Jesus will tell you that the road is exactly as he promised: narrow and hard.

In the Midst of Mystery

It's hard, not just because loving sacrificially as Jesus did is hard, but also because every minute of every day, we live in the midst of mystery. God is so much bigger than we are. If he weren't, he wouldn't be God, of course. God's ways, as Job discovered, are an unfathomable mystery. Life in this world raises so many questions, some which nag at us and drive us crazy. How can God care for the entire universe? Where is God, anyway? Some questions are like a sword, revealing deep pain: why do the innocent suffer?

And there are the moments of dryness. Those "dark nights of the soul," as St. John of the Cross called them, the times in which we go to Mass and try to pray but can't. Or when we send up our prayers, not able to imagine for a second that there is anyone there to hear them. Or that if there is, that someone must surely have better things to do than listen to our petty problems. Or when tragedy strikes us hard. Or a way of being, spiritually speaking, that previously brought us so much joy, in which everything seemed to just lock together and make sense, no longer works, and we flip back the journal pages from that time, reading words of certainty and joy, and think, Who was that person?

It can all make a person feel very lost.

It can all make a person feel as if Jesus is lost.

Watching Mary, listening to her, we might just find a way through. We search with her, through the bustling crowds going about their business, crowds ignorant of our pain or, if we venture to ask, unable to help. We travel down dead ends; we ask and ask again, hearing only, "Not here . . . no . . . not here."

We wonder if we will ever see him again. We remember the promise we heard long ago that was so real and life giving, now a promise that we cling to as we search, listening and hoping.

Then there he is. With her, we see him again. Relieved. A little bit annoyed. What was all of this trouble about? Was it really necessary? How could you do this to me?

Surely things will go back to normal now. But when Jesus speaks, something tells us that there will be a "new normal" now. Things have shifted slightly. Or perhaps they were always this way, but we just didn't know it.

It will be different for each of us, but every time we rediscover Christ, every time we find him again, even though he does not change, we do, and what we are called to do becomes more.

We find him again, in Jerusalem. Again and again, we find him about his Father's business.

Living in the culture and time that we do, our lives are defined by neat packaging, scientific answers, plans, schemas, and programs. Always programs for everything. Programs that will solve our problems and make everything crystal clear now and forever. We also live in an unending storm of information, the world at our fingertips at the click of a mouse.

It is noisy, it is busy, it is very smart and profitable.

But is it wise?

Mystery confronts us: Jesus found once again, in the Temple, inviting us to consider who he is and what his business might be and what we might have to do with it. When that mystery confronts us, do we stop, even for a moment, to listen, think, contemplate, and listen again?

Is there even room in our heads? Do we have the patience if the answer isn't evident right here and right now? Or do we simply give up and shop for something else, another program, another set of answers that seems to lay it all out so simply—for now?

Or, are we more like Mary?

Mary, who knew some things about her son—essential things, but mind-boggling things. Mary, who knew quite a bit, but was now being confronted with something new.

"His mother treasured all these things in her heart."

Mary's life is one of pondering, of being aware, of listening, of pulling things together within, of being patient, of allowing God the space to knit the answers within her. Luke tells us in the book of Acts, the second part of his gospel, that Mary was present at Pentecost, as the Spirit of understanding was poured out on the disciples. We noted before that Luke has a particular interest in illuminating the nature of discipleship. Part of that reality, as Luke describes the journey of the apostles, and here in Mary's life, means accepting that we don't understand everything here and now. In fact, we won't. There's just no way we can.

But in patience, we keep searching. And once we find even a glimmer, we listen, ponder, and follow. ✑

The Memorare

God's generosity to us, his rather stubborn and resistant children, is boundless.

There is, it seems, nothing God won't do to reach us. It's the history of salvation, from the people of Israel onward, as God creates us out of pure, passionate love and forgives us over and over again when we turn from him. Meeting us where we are, then calling us just a bit further along the road. Revealing to us the promises of joy and hope, giving us the strength to make the journey there, to feast at his table.

When we look at Jesus, the word-made-flesh, born a helpless child, pouring his blood out on the cross, it seems as if there isn't anything God won't do to bring us home to him.

The spiritual journeys of Christians through history, the staggering diversity of ways that the saints have sought and found peace in God, and the various movements through which the Spirit has worked to enlighten, nourish, and redeem make that clear. The sheer earthiness of it all, the openness, the accessibility of God. There are no secrets, no passwords, no hidden wisdom with God. Simply love. Love as you can, and then love some more—which you can, because God loved you first.

People who are intensely devoted to helping other souls find the joy of life in God know this. They also know that it's sometimes necessary to go to extremes to shake up the lost and open their eyes to how loved they are.

Fr. Claude Bernard was like that.

Fr. Bernard, or the "Poor Priest," as he was commonly known, lived in France in the seventeenth century. His life was about ministering to the poorest of the poor and especially criminals, the most unrepentant, hardened criminals.

At some point in his life, Fr. Bernard found a prayer. Perhaps he wrote it, or perhaps he just discovered it. To be sure, it was through his efforts that it became popular. It's called the *Memorare*:

> Remember, O most gracious Virgin Mary, that never was it known that anyone who fled to thy protection, implored thy help, or sought thy intercession was left unaided. Inspired with this confidence, I fly to thee, O Virgin of virgins, my Mother; to thee do I come; before thee I stand, sinful and sorrowful. O Mother of the Word Incarnate, despise not my petitions, but in thy mercy hear and answer me. Amen.

(The prayer is sometimes mistakenly attributed to St. Bernard of Clairvaux because of a misreading of prayer cards with the *Memorare* and "Fr. Bernard" printed on them.)

Fr. Bernard decided that this was the prayer that he would use in his efforts to reach the lost of the lost. He knew that if he could get them to pray this prayer, their hearts would be opened to the ready grace of God.

Fr. Bernard would do anything to get his charges to pray the *Memorare*. He went to such lengths that if one would refuse, he might physically stuff the slip of paper with the prayer written on it into the man's mouth. And believe it or not, this worked. Even on the scaffold, before an execution, one of Fr. Bernard's lost souls, moved by the priest's insistence that he make the prayer a part of his life, literally did pray it and, at the last minute, sought forgiveness for his sins and was reconciled to Christ.

It sounds a bit crazy, but is it really? Just think how resistant we can be to the truth, especially the truth that we are so deeply loved. What Fr. Bernard figured out is that there is something that even the hardest of hearts finds almost impossible to resist: the love of a mother.

If that is what it takes, Fr. Bernard knew, God can use it, for God can use anything to reach us—and does.

CHAPTER 8

The Miracle at Cana

[Mary] trusts unconditionally, indeed even in
the face of apparent rejection and rebuke, in the efficacy
of the Word of Jesus.
—Francis J. Moloney, *The Gospel of John*, 68

"They have no wine."

"Do whatever he tells you."

Mary speaks exactly twice in John's gospel, once to Jesus and then to a group of servants. She presents Jesus with a problem; then she turns and instructs the servants how to listen to him.

From Cana to our ears.

On the third day there was a wedding in Cana of Galilee, and the mother of Jesus was there. Jesus and his disciples had also been invited to the wedding. When the wine gave out, the mother of Jesus said to him, "They have no wine." And Jesus said to her, "Woman, what concern is that to you and to me? My hour has not yet come." His mother said to the servants, "Do whatever he tells you." Now standing there were six stone water jars for the Jewish rites of purification, each holding twenty or thirty gallons. Jesus said to them, "Fill the jars with water." And they filled them up to the brim. He said to them, "Now draw some out, and take it to the chief steward." So they took it. When the steward tasted the water that had become wine, and did not know where it came from (though the servants who had drawn the water knew), the steward called the bridegroom and said to him, "Everyone serves the good wine first, and then the inferior wine after the guests have become drunk. But you have kept the good wine until now." Jesus did this, the first of his signs, in Cana of Galilee, and revealed his glory; and his disciples believed in him. (John 2:1-11)

It seems silly to try to pick out a "best-known" miracle of Jesus, but if we were forced to, we would probably select this one. Everyone knows the story: a tough situation brought to Jesus, which he solves out of compassion for a distressed couple. Nice story, right?

Not quite. To think of the miracle at Cana as being about nothing more than Jesus reviving a nearly disastrous party is like saying that the multiplication of the loaves and the fishes (see John 6:4-14) is about methods of efficient festival maintenance. These are gospels, not bare factual narratives. And furthermore, this is John.

John's gospel is unique. Most scholars agree that it was written later than the three synoptic gospels. Much that is in the synoptic gospels is not in John, which makes sense if you consider that the others had been in circulation for a couple of decades by the time John was written. Why should the author repeat what was already written, circulated, and well-known in an era of scarce writing resources? He had his own recollections of Jesus to share:

This is the disciple who is testifying to these things and has written them, and we know that his testimony is true. But there are also many other things that Jesus did; if every one of them were written down, I suppose that the world itself could not contain the books that would be written. (John 21:24-25)

The first part of John's gospel is structured around "signs" or miracles. Through these signs, Jesus' identity as the Son of the Father is revealed, an identity that is fully made manifest in the second half of the gospel when Jesus' "hour" arrives, his crucifixion, the event in which we see God's radical love revealed through Jesus' sacrifice on the cross.

In Jesus' first sign, all of this is hinted at through rich, yet startlingly simple, imagery.

The Wedding Feast

The scene is Cana, a village traditionally believed to be about nine miles north of Galilee. In Jewish culture of the first century, a wedding feast continued for many days and involved the whole community. To run out of wine was a scandal and a shame, for in this culture, hospitality was a sacred obligation.

We don't know who was getting married. We don't know how they knew Mary or Jesus. All we know is that at some point the wine ran out and Mary told Jesus about it. What's interesting is that if you remove that crucial verse—verse four—the story reads very simply, as a clean and crisp story of a generously-motivated miracle, solving a critical problem.

But there is verse four. A rebuke, almost, from Jesus to his mother.

"Woman, what concern is that to you and to me? My hour has not yet come."

Mary doesn't respond as if she's been rebuked at all. She simply turns to the servants and tells them to do whatever Jesus tells them to do. Which they do. And then wine, the best wine, fills the jars.

Stepping back from Cana and looking at what comes before and after it in the gospel, we notice that nothing is random here, and there is more to see.

The first chapter of John's gospel begins with the great Prologue in which he describes Jesus as the *Logos* or "Word" of God, made flesh, pitching his tent among humanity. John the Baptist testifies, and the disciples are called.

And then immediately after all that, it is on to Cana.

What follows? More signs, including a second sign at Cana (see John 4:46-54). Encounters with various individuals, including a blind man and a Samaritan woman. All pointing to gradual revelations of who Jesus is and how various people respond to him.

What directly follows Cana, however, gives us a clue as to what Cana is really all about. Immediately after the wedding, Jesus travels to Capernaum and then to Jerusalem, where he clears the Temple of money changers. Right after that, he has an encounter and long conversation with Nicodemus, who is a Pharisee, and to whom Jesus talks about being "born from above"—baptism.

The sign at Cana introduces all of this, for the miracle is about more than jars of water. It's about Jesus replacing the old with the new—himself.

The waters jars aren't just random containers. They were, as John notes in 2:6, the jars filled with water for ritual washing. It is this water that Jesus transforms into a superabundance of the finest wine.

After this miracle, he travels to Jerusalem to cleanse the Temple of those who are defiling it.

In the Old Testament, banquets and an abundance of food and wine are signs of the fullness of God's kingdom:

MARY BEGINS THE CHURCH'S JOURNEY

At the end of the account of Jesus' first miracle, made possible by the firm faith of the Lord's Mother in her divine Son, the Evangelist John concludes: "and his disciples believed in him" (2:11). At Cana, Mary begins the Church's journey of faith, preceding the disciples and directing the servants' attention to Christ.

—Pope John Paul II, General Audience, March 5, 1997

At Cana, the Blessed Virgin once again showed her total availability to God. At the Annunciation she had contributed to the miracle of the virginal conception by believing in Jesus before seeing him; here, her trust in Jesus' as yet unrevealed power causes him to perform his "first sign," the miraculous transformation of water into wine.

—Pope John Paul II, General Audience, February 26, 1997

> On this mountain the LORD of hosts will make for
>   all peoples
>   a feast of rich food, a feast of well-aged wines,
>   of rich food filled with marrow, of well-aged wines
>   strained clear. (Isaiah 25:6)

When we look at the miracle at Cana, not just in light of what comes before but what comes afterward, we can see another dimension. Jesus' "hour" is the moment in which his glory is revealed as the word-made-flesh, as God's Son. That "hour" occurs on the cross, when Jesus' blood is poured out in love for us. This pouring out is something that we, those who have been born again by water and the spirit (see John 3:5), share every time we celebrate the Eucharist, the banquet of bread and wine.

Mary's Presence at Cana

And now, back to Mary. Mary is only brought into the picture twice in John's gospel, but she appears in places that we don't see in the other gospels. The miracle at Cana is only in John, and Mary's place at the foot of the cross is also explicitly noted only in John.

As is so often the case, we shouldn't take a relative absence for unimportance. Mary's presence at Cana is crucial, not only for what it says about her but for what it reveals to us about the nature of the Church.

First, look at how Mary is described. When we see her here and later at the cross, she is not called by her name. She is called the "mother of Jesus." It almost seems as if John, who emphasizes Jesus' identity as the word-made-flesh, is trying to help us see this relationship in its theological essence, apart from the personal identity of this woman. She is the one through whom Jesus' identification with humanity is most vividly expressed.

The word of God was made flesh in a mother.

Now what does this mother say to her Son? For some reason, rooted in her knowledge of her Son, Mary brings the problem to his attention: "They have no wine." Stepping back and looking at the bigger picture once again, we see a direct expression of the situation, which echoes the cry of the prophets from ages past:

> Therefore because you trample on the poor
>> and take from them levies of grain,
> you have built houses of hewn stone,
>> but you shall not live in them;
> you have planted pleasant vineyards,
>> but you shall not drink their wine. (Amos 5:11)

Again, it is not just about a potential social disaster. Through Mary's words, we hear of the neediness in which God's people find themselves, just as through her words in Luke, we hear of the promise of restoration, fulfillment, and joy.

Jesus' response is startling. There are various translations of his words in John 2:4. The New Revised Standard Version reads, "Woman, what concern is that to you and to me?" The New American translation, which Catholics hear at Mass, reads, "Woman, how does your concern affect me?" Both have the same impact. He puts her at a distance, indicating that he moves in response to God's timetable and no one else's.

This verse points not to any disrespect for his mother, but to one of John's major themes—the primacy of the relationship between Jesus and the Father.

What seems like a brush-off to us doesn't deter Mary in the least. She simply turns and tells the servants to "do whatever he tells you."

Note that we're given no sense that Mary had any idea at all what Jesus was actually going to do. For all we know, he's not going to do anything. Her words don't presume the miracle that comes. They are simple instructions: obey his word, who is the word-made-flesh.

John comes back to this point again and again. Jesus is the Word, the self-expression of God. What is our response?

It might be startling to think back through our lives or even simply the past week and consider what our response has actually been to the Word. Have we even tried to listen as we've made our decisions about matters great and small? Or have other voices caught our ear first?

If we do discern what the Word is saying to us through our consciences, our prayer, and our reading of Scripture, do we follow Mary's instruction and "do whatever he tells us"?

Or do we argue, rationalize, and sigh that we'll get more serious about letting Christ live in us later, but right now we can't, because there might be some sort of price to pay?

When I read the gospels, I am consistently struck by the power of small details, of the concentrated spiritual resonance in each verse. The miracle at Cana is just one more example of that. Mary, not even named, makes the briefest of appearances, yet reveals so much.

She reveals, first of all, her own role in the Church. Like a true friend, like an ever-vigilant mother, she perceives our needs and our emptiness, takes them, and intercedes for us. Second, she trusts. She obeys—and she instructs us to listen, trust, and obey as well.

Despite the forms into which popular Catholic devotion has veered at times, our appreciation of Mary is primarily not about her alone, but about what she reveals to us about her Son.

In the early Church, as various heretics questioned Jesus' full humanity, Mary was brought into the discussion again and again as evidence that he was, indeed, fully human. Every time we find ourselves wandering, wondering what it means to be a faithful disciple of Jesus, Mary stands there in the pages of the gospels, showing us so clearly, again and again: trust, listen, act.

ON THE DEVOTIONAL SIDE

Our Lady of . . .

From the earliest years, when they gathered up the remains of the martyrs and then gathered for prayer at their places of martyrdom and burial, Christians have been keenly aware of what we call the "communion of saints."

Jesus' victory over death shows us that the end of physical life is not the end. We on earth are joined with those in heaven, in praise, prayer, and the bonds of love that death can no longer break.

So just as we associate certain living persons with various places, events, and things, we do the same with the dead. We think of the young having a particular concern for the young, those who suffered from a certain illness or trouble with those experiencing the same on earth right now, and so on. We call them "patron saints"—friends in heaven who know what it is like to experience what we experience, and can help us through their prayers.

Mary, of course, is only one person, but her patronage has been called on in all sorts of circumstances and situations and in every country. Every culture, it seems, has a particular dimension of Mary. They honor and call on "Our Lady" or "Mother of . . ." because she is our lady, our mother. The center of these devotions is often an image of Mary that serves as a reminder of the constant, loving presence of God, and Mary's life as an expression of that love.

As we find to be the case constantly in Catholic spirituality, devotions to Mary are diverse and touch on every aspect of human life. There's something for everyone. These are some of the more popular and long-lasting examples:

Our Lady of Guadalupe

In 1517 the Blessed Virgin appeared to St. Juan Diego, an indigenous Mexican near modern-day Mexico City. As evidence of her presence and love, her image was miraculously left on Juan Diego's *tilma,* or cloak. The image is of a dark-skinned royal, noble figure, surrounded by roses and images that recall the "woman clothed with the sun" of Revelation 12. The *tilma* is exhibited in the Shrine of Our Lady of Guadalupe in Mexico City. She is patroness of the Americas and the unborn, and her feast day is December 12.

Our Lady of Prompt Succor and Our Lady of Perpetual Help

Mary, as Mother of the Church, is often turned to by those in need. Our Lady of Prompt Succor is a devotion nurtured for two hundred years in New Orleans by Ursuline nuns who first appealed for Mary's intercession for their school in the early nineteenth century. Our Lady of Perpetual Help is a devotion inspired by an icon from a Roman church that was lost after the French invaded Rome in 1812 but was found forty years later.

Our Lady of Lourdes

In 1858 Bernadette Soubirous, a sickly, illiterate French girl, experienced apparitions of the Blessed Virgin for several months in a grotto outside the village of Lourdes, during which Mary said, "I am the Immaculate Conception." Millions flock to Lourdes every year for prayer and healing. Our Lady of Lourdes is patroness of those suffering bodily ills, and her feast is celebrated on February 11.

Our Lady of Africa and Black Madonna Images

Our Lady of Africa, centered around a statue brought from France to Algiers in the nineteenth century, provides a continuing focus for the difficult lives of Christians in North Africa. The dark-skinned statue stands in the Basilica of Our Lady of Africa and is known as the "Consolation of the Afflicted."

Black Madonnas—images of Mary with dark skin—are found throughout Europe. Sometimes the reasons for the darkened skin seem to be the accidental result of age or smoke damage, but in other cases the dark skin is purposeful, perhaps as an expression of the song of the bride in Song of Songs, who says, "I am black and beautiful" (1:5).

Our Lady of Czestochowa is the most well known of the "Black Madonna" images of Mary. Centuries old, kept in a monastery in Jasna Gora, Poland, the image has represented the protection and safety given to us by Jesus through the prayers of his mother.

CHAPTER 9

Mary at the Foot of the Cross

*Just so, because [on Calvary] the Blessed Virgin truly suffered
the pangs of a woman in childbirth, and because
in her Son's Passion she gave birth to the salvation of us all,
she is clearly the Mother of us all.*
—Rupert of Deutz, "On John," in
Mary in the Middle Ages, 130

It is another iconic image etched into our collective spiritual memory, alongside the nativity and the crucifixion itself: Mary at the foot of the cross.

Images don't become iconic because someone decides they should. No, the images that evoke a strong emotional and spiritual response that resonates with the deepest parts of human experience are those that cross cultures and time and stay with us. These are the images that never seem to lose their meaning.

So what is it about this one?

We see what we saw at the beginning: a mother and a child. But this time, the situation is radically different. The hope of the Madonna with the baby on her lap seems shattered as she stands at the base of the cross, watching her son die, unable to do a thing to stop it, powerless to end his pain. Just as we can identify with the hope and possibility, we also know what it is like to stand in the presence of suffering and darkness, our hearts broken for those we love, willing to trade our own suffering for theirs in an instant, if it were only possible.

No, we can't take our eyes off the mother and her son.

John's Witness

This heartrending image is only found in the gospel of John. The synoptic writers describe women gathered at the cross, most notably, the women who had followed Jesus "from Galilee," ministering to him, including Mary Magdalene and some of the same women who would discover the empty tomb (Matthew 27:55-56; Mark 15:40-41; Luke 23:49).

Why is this? It is impossible to know, but one of the things we always must remember is that the evangelists highlight incidents from the life of Jesus for a purpose. So in the three synoptic gospels, there is clearly a connection between the faithful presence of the women at the cross and the fact that these women, who remained with Jesus to the end, are the first witnesses of the risen Christ.

John is making connections, as well—theological and spiritual connections.

Meanwhile, standing near the cross of Jesus were his mother, and his mother's sister, Mary the wife of Clopas, and Mary Magdalene. When Jesus saw his mother and the disciple whom he loved standing beside her, he said to his mother, "Woman, here is your son." Then he said to the disciple, "Here is your mother." And from that hour the disciple took her into his own home. (John 19:25-27)

This is the second mention of Mary in the gospel of John. The first was the wedding at Cana. There, as here, you'll see that

Mary is described in the same way: as "mother," rather than by her name. Jesus refers to her in the same way in both accounts: as "woman."

This scene has provided rich food for thought through the centuries. Theologians have mined the succinct words of Jesus for their implications about Mary and the Church. Spiritual writers have listened to Jesus' words and heard a sense of a new relationship between Mary and the rest of us.

On a most practical level, what most of us hear is an expression of a son's love and concern for his mother. We can assume, along with most of the rest of Christian observers throughout history, that Joseph had died by this time. In addition, we can see, as writers from antiquity have deduced, that Jesus' placing his mother in the "beloved disciple's" care is an indication that she would be alone without Jesus. There were no brothers or sisters to take her in.

Beyond that, there is enormous spiritual resonance in this narrative, amazing because it is so brief, but perhaps not so amazing because it is John, who had decades to ponder over what he and the witnesses whose testimony he knew had seen and heard.

First, we have to go back to Cana. In the story of this first of Jesus' "signs" or manifestations of his identity as the Son of God the Father, Jesus referred to Mary as "woman." Then he asked her, rhetorically perhaps, what this situation had to do with him, establishing a sort of distance between God's ways of doing things and our ways, and echoing the same question he had asked his parents during the finding at the Temple.

Jesus went on to clarify (a bit) at Cana, saying that his "hour" had not yet come. John makes clear throughout his gospel that the "hour" was the death of Jesus on the cross. This is the "hour," because it is the time when Jesus' identity would be fully revealed as the Son of God the Father, who is love. "For God so loved the world that he gave his only Son, so that everyone who believes in him may not perish but may have eternal life" (John 3:16).

What has led up to this hour? What is to come afterward? If we scan through the gospel of John, we see that there is more to this story than simply Jesus and God the Father.

Throughout the gospel, as Jesus works his signs, encounters individuals and their varied responses to him, and confronts the Temple authorities, we can see a new people of God being slowly but surely formed. Jesus, as the Word, the Light, the Bread, the Living Water, and the Shepherd (all prominent images in John), comes into the world and gathers a new people, a new community, a new family of God.

How do you become a part of this family? You are baptized in water and the spirit (see John 3). You listen and let your life be guided by the Shepherd, the Light and the Word. You are fed by the Living Bread from Heaven. And you serve one another in love, as the Son poured out himself in love (see John 3:13-17).

In Cana, Mary showed herself to be the perfect disciple, not because she was related to Jesus by blood, but because she obeyed his word and called others to do the same. From almost the beginning of Christian theological contemplation, many have seen in Mary, especially in the rather iconic way of speaking of her as "woman," an understanding of what Jesus is doing by reflecting back on Genesis, creation and fall.

Many believed, picking up on Paul's reflection on sin and death coming into the world through a man and then being defeated by a man (Romans 5:11-15), that Mary was like a new Eve. The fall that had come in part through the yes of a *woman*—Eve—was being turned around and defeated through the yes of another *woman*—Mary. This is why Jesus' calling Mary "woman," an

BEHOLD YOUR SON

Of the essence of motherhood is the fact that it concerns the person. Motherhood always establishes a unique and unrepeatable relationship between two people: between mother and child and between child and mother. Even when the same woman is the mother of many children, her personal relationship with each one of them is of the very essence of motherhood. For each child is generated in a unique and unrepeatable way, and this is true both for the mother and for the child. Each child is surrounded in the same way by that maternal love on which are based the child's development and coming to maturity as a human being.

It can be said that motherhood "in the order of grace" preserves the analogy with what "in the order of nature" characterizes the union between mother and child. In the light of this fact it becomes easier to understand why in Christ's testament on Golgotha his Mother's new motherhood is expressed in the singular, in reference to one man: "Behold your son."

—Pope John Paul II, *Redemptoris Mater,* 45

unheard-of way for a son to address his mother, isn't understood by Christians as being disrespectful, but rather as being a sign of the deeper meaning of this relationship of mother to son and, by extension, to all of us.

So now, at the "hour" of Jesus' glorification, the faithful woman and the beloved, faithful disciple stand at the foot of the cross. Jesus' last act before dying is to entrust his mother and the beloved disciple to each other. A simpler translation of his words would be, "Look: your son" and "Look: your mother."

In the midst of sorrow and mystery, the shape of the new family of God is somehow made clear. For as we know, this mystery, this glorification, this hour is about love. It is God's love that brought the world into being and God's love that saves this same world as it plummets into darkness, turning inexplicably from the light, so tragically forgetful of where true, lasting joy lies. The community of disciples, the family joined by water and the Spirit, nourished by the bread of life, living in love, is the presence of that light, God's light, in the darkness.

In that family, we are put into each other's care, to "look" at each other in a new way, shaped by sacrificial love.

In that family, Mary matters.

In fact, in that family, in that community, Mary stands at the center, entrusted to the care of the family, with the family entrusted to her care as well.

"Look: your mother."

As scholar Francis Moloney puts it: "The maternal role of the Mother of Jesus in the new family of Jesus is established at the Cross."[13]

Before we move on, thinking, "Yes, yes, family of God—got it," we might pause and think about those who surround us when we go to Mass, the millions around the world who are our brothers and sisters by baptism. Do we have any real, deep sense that we are actually in each other's care, that this really is a new, radical identity we share, or is it all simply about sharing a room with folks who happen to share some of our same views . . . and then moving on?

Mary's Suffering

Nothing is more painful than the suffering of one's own child. Those of us who are parents know the dreadful sense of helplessness, the fear, the grief, and even the prayer that if it were possible, the cup would be passed on to us, and we would gladly, gratefully drink from it instead. There is something unique about that triad of parent, child, and suffering. The deepest fear of most parents involves their children's suffering and death. There is almost something perverse and wrong about children preceding their parents in death. That's just not the way it's supposed to be.

We may respond similarly to the suffering of anyone we love and if we are particularly saintly, which we are called to be, to the suffering of anyone we meet, or even the knowledge of the suffering of any person, at any time, anywhere. Some wonder why contemplative religious spend so much time in prayer. How could anyone do that? Is there really that much to pray about?

Well, read the newspapers. There's your answer.

The suffering of others often presents us with dilemmas, discomfort, and questions. Someone I know and love is suffering. How should I act? What should I do? What can I do to help, even though it seems as if nothing really can be done, whether that suffering is physical pain that is beyond medication or mental and spiritual pain that is beyond our reach.

The question is especially keen today, in this world where suffering and its causes are pushed into closets, behind antiseptic hospital and nursing home doors, and everyone is encouraged to be as happy, cheerful, and productive as possible. If it gets hard, well just buy something. That should help. And please . . . stop feeling so bad about yourself.

Flannery O'Connor, the great American writer who was also a devout Catholic, and who also suffered and died from the immunological disease lupus, once wrote that being sick is like being in a foreign country. This is true of any kind of physical, psychological, or spiritual suffering as well. There are borders, it seems. Maybe even fences and the border patrol.

So how can we help?

Look at Mary.

Be present. Don't hide, don't shut doors, and don't turn away, convinced that there is nothing you could do or that there is no need for you.

Love, after all, is what John tells us over and over that Jesus is about. Love requires, first of all, presence. Sometimes our presence can lead to action, but sometimes presence is enough.

Of course, presence is hard. It is horrible to watch someone suffer; it is even worse when our hands are tied. Who wouldn't be tempted to run away? Even if we're not in the situation of the disciples, who literally feared for their lives, remaining with the suffering can make us fear for our lives in another way, as we face our own future, as we face the possibilities of pain that exist for all of us, as we are reminded of the suffering we may have survived in the past.

But given all of that, what is really the alternative to presence? It's running away, denial, closed eyes. It is fear.

We don't know what went through Mary's mind as she watched her Son suffer and die. We can guess, and writers through history have used their imaginations to describe what she might have been feeling. A minor but intriguing theme of some medieval spiritual writing was that as she watched Jesus die, Mary experienced the birth pangs she had been spared thirty-three years before.

But it's hard to say what she felt beyond the normal pain of a mother watching her son unjustly executed and the extraordinary pain of a sword through her heart as she went over and over the angel's promises so long ago.

Jesus said that whenever we encounter suffering, we encounter him (see Matthew 25:31-46). So it stands to reason that when we are present with suffering, we are present at the cross with Mary at our side. We watch her and we learn how to be present, which means how to love, simply and deeply.

We are in each other's care. Empowered by love, we can be present—with Mary at our side.

ON THE DEVOTIONAL SIDE

Mary's Sorrow

We see so much of our own human experience in Mary. We see our wonder, our faith, our vocation, our joy, and our sorrow.

We Christians have found contemplating Mary's sorrow at Jesus' death helpful for our spiritual journeys, not because we are masochists but because we are realists, and Christianity is a profoundly realistic faith. It embraces every part of life because life is God's, and he is present in every part of this journey. Some religions declare suffering to be an illusion. Our own popular culture encourages us to just try to ignore or distract ourselves from suffering. Christianity does none of these. It approaches suffering as a mystery in which God is found.

Mary's sorrows have given Christians a way to understand suffering, as they stand with Mary at the cross, join their own particular sorrows to hers, and wait in hope for the resurrection. Two of the many expressions of Mary's sorrows are found in the devotion of the Seven Sorrows and in the hymn *Stabat Mater*.

The Seven Sorrows

John's description of Mary's presence at the cross, although simple and spare, inspired contemplation from Christianity's early years. The devotion developed more fully, beginning in the fourteenth century as various mystics and spiritual writers emerged with various lists of Mary's seven sorrows. Seven was the number traditionally associated with completeness or perfection, but it also corresponds to the number of daily prayer periods in the Liturgy of the Hours.

In the thirteenth century, the Servite Order embraced Mary's sorrow as their central devotion. They developed what is called the "Servite Chaplet" or "Servite Rosary," which is a unique rosary that has, instead of five sets of ten beads separated by single beads, seven sets of seven beads separated by single beads. There are variations in praying the Servite Chaplet, but in general, one prays a Hail Mary for each of the seven closely-set beads, reflecting on one of the Seven Sorrows during the prayer:

1. The prophecy of Simeon (Luke 2:34-35)
2. The flight into Egypt (Matthew 2:13-21)
3. The loss of Jesus for three days (Luke 2:41-50)
4. The ascent to Calvary (John 19:17)
5. The crucifixion and death of Jesus (John 19:18-30)
6. Jesus Taken Down from the Cross (John 19:39-40)
7. Jesus Laid in the Tomb (John 19:39-42)

The Seven Sorrows is a scripturally based prayer, in which we are drawn into the suffering of Christ, and through which we unite our own suffering to his in sorrow for our sins and in the trust of forgiveness. The feast of Our Lady of Sorrows is celebrated on September 15, the day after the feast of the Holy Cross.

Stabat Mater

The *Stabat Mater*, which means "Mother Standing," is a sequence or hymn that originated in the thirteenth century. Most of us are familiar with it from its use during the Stations of the Cross. It is sung or recited on September 15, the Feast of Our Lady of Sorrows. It has been set to music by hundreds of composers over the centuries. The following excerpt helps us see its appeal. As we observe and enter into Mary's love and sadness, we pray that we will grow in our own love for Jesus:

At the cross her station keeping,
Stood the mournful Mother weeping,
Close to Jesus to the last.

Through her heart, his sorrow sharing,
All his bitter anguish bearing,
Now at length the sword had pass'd.

Oh, how sad and sore distress'd
Was that Mother highly blest
Of the sole-begotten One!

Christ above in torment hangs;
She beneath beholds the pangs
Of her dying glorious Son.

Is there one who would not weep,
Whelm'd in miseries for deep
Christ's dear Mother to behold?

Bruis'd, derided, curs'd, defil'd
She beheld her tender child
All with bloody scourges rent.

For the sins of his own nation
Saw him hand in desolation
Till his spirit forth he sent.
O thou Mother! Fount of love!
Touch my spirit from above,
Make my heart with thine accord.

Virgin of all virgins best,
Listen to my found request.
Let me share thy grief divine.

CHAPTER 10

A Woman Clothed with the Sun

It may seem like just a single moment in your life, but right now, every moment, a river is coursing.

We can usually only see it in retrospect. We realize that as we were making a certain decision, this factor from the past was pushing us one way, another factor was shading our thinking in another way, hopes for a particular future were inspiring us, and in the midst of it all, coincidence, happenstance, and any number of other factors were also at work. All kinds of things are going on, including, perhaps, a plan, greater and deeper than we could have realized then or even grasp now.

This dynamic between our ways and God's, the accidental and the purposeful, the hope that glimmers through questions, uncertainty, and even darkness is the complicated, enticing mystery at the heart of the life God has given us. And given to Mary, because she is one of us.

But what of the life to come? What, in the end, does it all mean?

Again, Mary gives us a glimpse.

The Woman in the Book of Revelation

Revelation is a strange, mysterious book, read in various ways throughout history and put to various theological uses. Exploding with symbolism, it is not a book for casual reading.

The form of the book is "apocalyptic," a term derived from a Greek word meaning "unveiling." Apocalyptic literature is marked by a sense that great events playing out in heaven are reflected in earthly events, and those earthly events usually involve suffering, but ultimately hope, for believers.

You can find examples of apocalyptic literature in the Old Testament, such as the book of Daniel, as well as in works that were circulating in the centuries before Jesus' life and ministry. These writings emerged as the Jewish people experienced suffering and oppression at the hands of greater powers, from the Babylonians to the Greeks and finally, the Romans.

The book of Revelation in the New Testament echoes the themes of celestial warfare, suffering, and hope we find in Jewish apocalyptic writings. Scholars are divided as to the time of its composition. It is most commonly dated to the end of the first century during the reign of the Emperor Domitian (A.D. 81–96), but various ancient sources and a growing body of scholarly opinion today date it during the reign of Nero (A.D. 54–68). One of the reasons for a reconsideration of the dating is that Domitian did not actually systematically persecute Christians, while Nero did, and suffering under intense persecution is the constant background for the book of Revelation.

The author of Revelation identifies himself from the very beginning and repeatedly throughout as "John." Again, the identity of this John is disputed and has been for centuries. Is he the apostle John, the evangelist John (presuming they are not the same person), or another "John of Patmos" who is neither of these?

No one really knows. What we do know is that the author of this book was deeply committed to Christ and was a leader of the Christian community with enough authority to be able to write this book as a letter to the "seven churches" of Asia Minor, which he seems to have overseen.

The content of the book of Revelation is too complex to summarize here, but we have to say something in order to set the passage that refers to Mary in context. What precedes these verses are eleven chapters in which we see heaven, the Lamb enthroned, and a scroll with seven seals, each of which are opened with great and difficult consequences for life on earth. And then, in chapter 12, we meet a woman:

> A great portent appeared in heaven: a woman clothed with the sun, with the moon under her feet, and on her head a crown of twelve stars. She was pregnant and was crying out in birth pangs, in the agony of giving birth. Then another portent appeared in heaven: a great red dragon, with seven heads and ten horns, and seven diadems on his heads. His tail swept down a third of the stars of heaven and threw them to the earth. Then the dragon stood before the woman who was about to bear a child, so that he might devour her child as soon as it was born. And she gave birth to a son, a male child, who is to rule all the nations with a rod of iron. But her child was snatched away and taken to God and to his throne; and the woman fled into the wilderness, where she has a place prepared by God, so that there she can be nourished for one thousand two hundred sixty days. . . .
>
> [A battle ensues between Michael and the dragon. The dragon is defeated and thrown to earth.]
>
> So when the dragon saw that he had been thrown down to the earth, he pursued the woman who had given birth to the male child. But the woman was given the two wings of the great eagle, so that she could fly from the serpent

into the wilderness, to her place where she is nourished for a time, and times, and half a time. Then from his mouth the serpent poured water like a river after the woman, to sweep her away with the flood. But the earth came to the help of the woman; it opened its mouth and swallowed the river that the dragon had poured from his mouth. Then the dragon was angry with the woman, and went off to make war on the rest of her children, those who keep the commandments of God and hold the testimony of Jesus.

Then the dragon took his stand on the sand of the seashore. (Revelation 12:1-6, 13-18)

The one temptation we must avoid in interpreting any passage from Revelation, including this one, is to approach it linearly, with a single dimension of symbolism, thinking, "Well, this means that, and nothing else, and leads to the next set of events."

Revelation isn't like that. There are layers of symbolism here, and the writing has what someone has called a "plasticity." Like life, each detail carries a number of meanings—any number of meanings.

The woman's appearance in the midst of earth's turmoil tells us she is associated with Israel and the cosmos God has made. She is clothed with the sun, as God is described in Psalm 104:2 as "wrapped in light." Her crown of twelve stars reminds us of the twelve tribes of Israel, as well as Joseph's dream of the sun, the moon, and the eleven stars bowing down to him (see Genesis 37:9).

The woman's cries are not just cries of physical pain, they are the "cries" to God that Israel has uttered for generations (Psalm 22:5), yearning for God's saving presence. The male child who will rule calls to mind the expectations voiced by the prophets, the eagle calls to mind the protection of God, described as "eagles' wings" (Isaiah 40:31), and the desert calls to mind the role that the desert has played in Israel's history as a place of refuge and stability.

Of course, the dragon's pursuit of the woman cannot help but remind us of Eve:

> "I will put enmity between you and the woman, and between your offspring and hers; he will strike your head, and you will strike his heel." (Genesis 3:15)

Finally, who could contemplate this vision of an evil entity pursuing a mother and her child—who is "snatched up" and taken to God's throne—and then pursuing the woman's "children," and not think of Mary, her son, and the Church?

The Assumption of Mary

The assumption of Mary is simply the teaching that Mary has been "assumed" or "taken" into heaven, body and soul. She enjoys now what all disciples hope for—the resurrection of the body, life eternal in the presence of God.

Although the assumption was not formally defined as Catholic doctrine until 1950 by Pope Pius XII, it was widely believed since ancient times. We find the original articulation of this belief in the Eastern Church. This isn't surprising because the East is where Christianity began and, for the first few centuries, where most theological conversations were taking place. In addition, from early on, Eastern Christians nurtured a strong devotion to Mary, in which her status in heaven reflects the Eastern understanding of salvation as a sharing in the life of God. The Eastern celebration of this event is called the "Dormition" or "falling asleep."

Eastern Christians believe that Mary did die and that Jesus took her body to heaven, leaving an empty tomb.

Western thinking about the assumption developed and flowered over the course of centuries. The feast was celebrated in Rome by the early eighth century. The formal definition of the ancient belief was articulated by Pius XII: "The Immaculate Virgin . . . when the course of her earthly life was finished, was taken up body and soul into heavenly glory."[14] What is left open in this definition is the question of whether Mary actually experienced death. Theologians debated that question, and still do, since death is one of the curses humanity experiences as the result of the fall. Theologians consider whether Mary, freed from original sin, would have experienced the consequence of death. Pope John Paul II, however, articulates the predominant view when he says, "To share in Christ's Resurrection, Mary had first to share in his death."[15] In the end, what the assumption means is that Christ's victory over death can be seen in Mary. What she enjoys now, in the presence of the Lord, awaits us as well.

So the woman of Revelation 12 is really all of these: she is Israel, Eve, the Church, and Mary. Catholic interpretation of this passage has reflected this depth for hundreds of years, as theologians and spiritual writers have interpreted it in light of the understanding, so clear in Jesus' words to Mary and the beloved disciple at the cross, that Mary and the Church are intimately identified with each other. In birthing the body of Christ, Mary births the Church, a church that she watches in its suffering and with which she suffers.

The image of Mary as a woman "clothed in the sun" certainly has power and has a place in Christian iconography. It is also important in Catholic and Orthodox understandings of Mary's place in heaven. But the image is also so complex that it serves

Mary Shared in Christ's Death

It is true that in Revelation death is presented as a punishment for sin. However, the fact that the Church proclaims Mary free from original sin by a unique divine privilege does not lead to the conclusion that she also received physical immortality. The Mother is not superior to the Son who underwent death, giving it a new meaning and changing it into a means of salvation.

Involved in Christ's redemptive work and associated in his saving sacrifice, Mary was able to share in his suffering and death for the sake of humanity's Redemption. What Severus of Antioch says about Christ also applies to her: "Without a preliminary death, how could the Resurrection have taken place?" To share in Christ's Resurrection, Mary had first to share in his death.

—Pope John Paul II, General Audience, June 25, 1997

to enrich our understanding even beyond this identification to help us see God's gift of Mary as the Mother of the Church—as our mother.

As we've seen throughout this book, Mary is a powerful presence in our lives as individuals and as a Christian community because in her we see the promise God holds out to all of us. We see that our yes—our *fiat*—matters. God moves and redeems in the midst of the most fundamental human mysteries of pregnancy and childbirth, using creation to re-create, to save.

In our presence to one another, we bear and welcome Christ. Our love of God and neighbor is part of the cosmic course of history. In welcoming the light of Christ, in celebrating his justice and passionate love, we are part of something astonishing and miraculous because it is God's work in the world, through us. The heart of discipleship is seeking Christ and, once we find him, listening and following his word. Suffering happens, and in the suffering of every person is Christ, to whom we are called to be quietly, lovingly present.

This is Mary's life. It is our life as well, lived, not alone, but under the care of a most loving mother, the gift of a most loving and understanding God.

Holy Mary,
Mother of God,
pray for us sinners,
now and at the hour of our death.
Amen.

Notes

1. *Akathistos* Hymn, *Internet Medieval Sourcebook*, ed. Paul Halsall, accessed at http://www.fordham.edu/halsall/source/akathis.html.

2. Joseph Ratzinger, "'Hail, Full of Grace': Elements of Marian Piety according to the Bible," in *Mary: The Church at the Source* by Joseph Ratzinger and Hans Urs von Balthasar (San Francisco: Ignatius Press, 2005), 64.

3. Article on the "Hail Mary" in the 1917 edition of the *Catholic Encyclopedia*, accessed at http://www.newadvent.org/cathen/07110b.htm.

4. Riccardo Barile, "Reflections on *Rosarium Virginis Mariae,*" *L'Osservatore Romano*, Weekly Edition in English (January, 22, 2003), 4.

5. Article on "Carem," in the 1917 edition of the *Catholic Encyclopedia*, accessed at http://www.newadvent.org/cathen/03345b.htm.

6. Benedict XVI, Encyclical Letter, *Deus Caritas Est*, 41, accessed at http://www.vatican.va.

7. Ratzinger, "'Hail, Full of Grace': Elements of Marian Piety according to the Bible,", 75.

8. John Paul II, Apostolic Letter, *Rosarium Virginis Mariae,* 11, accessed at http://www.vatican.va.

9. Caryll Houselander, *The Reed of God* (Allen, Texas: Christian Classics, 1944), 44–45.

10. Houselander, 46.

11. Dante, *Paradiso*, 23, 71–75.

12. St. Ephrem of Syria, *Hymns on the Nativity*, in *Ephrem the Syrian: Hymns*, Classics of Western Spirituality (New York: Paulist Press, 1989), 100.

13. Francis J. Moloney, SDB, *The Gospel of John*, Sacra Pagina Series, vol. 4 (Collegeville, MN: Liturgical Press, 1998), 504.

14. As quoted in the *Catechism of the Catholic Church*, 966.

15. Pope John Paul II, General Audience, June 25, 1997, accessed at http://www.vatican.va.

Acknowledgments

Excerpts from the English translation of the *Catechism of the Catholic Church* for use in the United States of America, copyright © 1994, United States Catholic Conference, Inc.—Libreria Editrice Vaticana. Used with permission.

Selections from Proclus of Contantinople, Ephrem the Syrian, Pseudo-Chrysostom, Hilary of Poitiers, and St. Jerome taken from *Mary and the Fathers of the Church*, ed. Luigi Gambero (San Francisco: Ignatius Press, 1999). Used by permission of the publisher.

Selections by Hans Urs von Balthasar and Joseph Ratzinger taken from *Mary: The Church at the Source* (San Francisco: Ignatius Press, 2005). Used by permission of the publisher.

Selections by Ambrose Autpert and Rupert of Deutz taken from *Mary in the Middle Ages*, ed. Luigi Gambero (San Francisco: Ignatius Press, 2005). Used by permission of the publisher.

"The Quickening of St. John the Baptist," *The Collected Poems of Thomas Merton*, copyright © 1949 by Our Lady of Gethsemani Monastery. Reprinted by permission of New Directions Publishing Corp.

Bibliography

De Montfort, St. Louis. *True Devotion to the Blessed Virgin*. Bay Shore, New York: Montfort Publications, 1984.

Ephrem the Syrian: Hymns; tr. Kathleen F. McVey; Classics of Western Spirituality. New York: Paulist Press, 1989.

Houselander, Caryll. *The Reed of God*. Allen, Texas: Christian Classics, 1944.

Mary and the Fathers of the Church; ed. Luigi Gambero. San Francisco: Ignatius Press, 1999.

Mary in the Middle Ages; ed. Luigi Gambero. San Francisco: Ignatius Press, 2005.

Merton, Thomas. *The Collected Poems of Thomas Merton*. New York: New Directions Publishing Corporation, 1980.

Moloney, Francis J., SDB. *The Gospel of John*; Sacra Pagina Series, vol. 4. Collegeville, MN: The Liturgical Press, 1998.

Ratzinger, Joseph and Hans Urs von Balthasar. *Mary: The Church at the Source*. San Francisco: Ignatius Press, 2005.

Ratzinger, Joseph. *Images of Hope: Meditations on Major Feasts*. San Francisco: Ignatius Press, 2006.